Bicycling® Magazine's Guide to

BIKE TOURING

Bicycling Magazine's Guide to
BIKE TOURING

Everything You Need to Know
to Travel Anywhere on a Bike

Doug Donaldson

RODALE

Bicycling is a registered trademark of Rodale Inc.

Printed in the United States of America
Rodale Inc. makes every effort to use acid-free ♾, recycled paper ♲.

Book design by Gavin Robinson
Photography credits appear on page 223.

Library of Congress Cataloging-in-Publication Data

Donaldson, Doug.
    Bicycling magazine's guide to bike touring : everything you need to know to travel any- where on a bike / Doug Donaldson.
        p.   cm.
    Includes index.
    ISBN-13 978–1–57954–862–9 paperback
    ISBN-10 1–57954–862–8 paperback
    1. Bicycle touring.   I. Title.
    GV1044.D66   2005
    796.6'4—dc22   2004027351

Distributed to the trade by Holtzbrinck Publishers

2 4 6 8 10 9 7 5 3   paperback

Bicycling.

We inspire and enable people to improve their lives and the world around them

For more of our products visit **rodalestore.com** or call 800-848-4735

Notice

The information in this book is meant to supplement, not replace, proper cycling training. Bicycle touring poses some inherent risks. The editors and publisher advise readers to take full responsibility for their safety and know their limits. Before following the advice in this book, be sure that your equipment is well-maintained, and do not take risks beyond your level of experience, aptitude, training, and fitness. The exercise and dietary advice in this book is not intended as a substitute for any exercise routine or dietary regimen that may have been prescribed by your doctor. As with all exercise and dietary programs, you should get your doctor's approval before beginning.

Mention of specific companies, organizations, or authorities in this book does not imply endorsement by the author or publisher, nor does mention of specific companies, organizations, or authorities imply that they endorse this book, its author, or the publisher.

Internet addresses and telephone numbers given in this book were accurate at the time it went to press.

This, my first book, is dedicated to my children,
Jeremy, Matthew, Katie, and Cassie,
and to wherever their adventures take them.

Contents

Contents

Acknowledgments

First and foremost, credit for this book must go to the *Bicycling* magazine readers, editors, and writers I worked with during my 4 years as an editor there. Along with sharing an enthusiastic joy of riding, readers also often shared their riding tips and experiences, many of which are incorporated in these pages.

I had the pleasure of working with some of the most experienced and knowledgeable editors and writers who've ever clicked in a pedal. A special thanks, indeed, to executive editor Bill Strickland, who many years ago plunged me into the sport by giving me a Stumpjumper that I still ride. He pushed me to become a better writer, editor, and cyclist.

While compiling each chapter, I quickly realized how much credit for information in this book should go to *Bicycling* writers Joe Kurmaskie, the former touring columnist, and Selene Yeager, the magazine's Fitness Chick. I'd also like to give a nod of the helmet to my riding buddies Stan Zukowski and Andrew Stanten, who keep me motivated and put up with my bleary-eyed grumbling on weekend morning rides.

Finally, thanks must go to Sports Group book editors Leah Flickinger, who signed me up for this ride, and Kathryn C. LeSage, who helped get me in gear. And, finally, thanks to Liesa Goins for kicking my butt to finish the book and for all our adventures yet to come.

Introduction

Two wheels can help you make memories of a lifetime

On a bike tour, the world unfolds in ways that you never expect but that you appreciate and savor long after you're back home. You ride yourself into spontaneous conversations with locals. You likely meet loads of folks eager to offer suggestions on restaurants to eat at and places to stay, from charming inns to hidden four-star dives. More frequently than you'd imagine, your new friends invite you in for a home-cooked dinner and offer a spare bedroom for the night.

The next day, you pull up to homespun roadside fruit stands that make you wonder how you will ever again eat a store-bought peach. Or maybe you take an extrasensory taste of a crisp Chardonnay or full-bodied Cabernet during a wine-country tour. Vacation rides reveal such pleasant surprises around every corner.

Rolling outside on a bike knocks you out of your routine and can even alter the way you see the world. Everything's possible when you're seeing the world from a bike seat—even changing your life. Sure, a tour is an escape, but oddly, even as you're getting away, you can find yourself when there's nothing to think about but open road or a winding trail.

No doubt, the slower pace but more challenging effort of a bike tour—whether it's your first one or a regular monthly escape—can be good for your body, mind, and spirit. Pushing those legs and lungs fuel the mind and boost the soul. Seeing sights only possible by bike taps into unknown energy that keeps you pedaling when you might otherwise feel too tired.

Best of all, on a bike tour, your problems and stress disappear. You're too engaged in riding the bike—watching the road for bumps, checking out scenery, thinking about the next stop, monitoring your body—to worry about much else. This full engagement is the hidden pleasure of cycling. You put your body and mind to one purpose. It builds self-esteem. You excavate stress. Plus, you feel good about enjoying the postride hours, whether they feature a guiltless bowl of ice cream or simply the most honest conversation you've experienced in months.

The main reason the world unzips on a tour: the bicycle itself. This amazing transportation device and discovery machine can move you from place to place without making you feel like you've skipped anything in between. The experience, the pace of a bike tour explains its increasing allure to cyclists worldwide. You move with life, live with it. When you are riding at 15 miles an hour, it's hard to miss things.

Bike touring offers options for everyone. If you're by yourself, you can wander at will, not obligated by a schedule, and can take all the side trips you want. Even when touring with others, it really doesn't matter when you roll into camp or a hotel, so don't feel pressured. Your tour might stay relatively close to home, pedaling to a neighboring town or discovering the local wholesale market district that you typically pass in your car at 40 miles per hour with barely a whiff of the fresh flowers or the morning catch of fish. Or you could discover a whole new state (Vermont for fall colors) or country (Italy, of course, remains a popular cycling destination) that has long been on your wish list.

No matter your destination, there are guided bike tours for every fitness level, even if you are a just-beginning-to-get-back-in-shape rider. Your body will be challenged, but the main obstacle is juggling your schedule—not your luggage, because guided tours take care of the planning and the transporting of bags. You simply need to pick a tour that conforms to your time constraints, budget, fitness level, willingness to camp, or aversion to bugs. You can indulge yourself in high-end luxury tours, staying at the finest lodgings. Or you can pound it out across the country, living campsite to campsite. The amount of planning is flexible, too. You can plan every detail yourself and haul 40 pounds of gear over the Rockies. Or you can simply show up with a touring company and pedal where they point you without even worrying about finishing a day's ride, since support vans are ready to sweep you from town to town if needed.

Trouble is, when it gets right down to hopping on the bike, John Lennon was right: Life is what happens when you are busy making other plans. We all experience it: the feeling that we don't get outside enough, that the season slipped away from us, that we have to wait until next time to get it right—and get outdoors. A bike tour positively and restoratively blocks out time from the rest of your life. What's more, bike touring is exploration. It might be only an hour—but more likely a day, weekend, or week—but it will be a full sensory experience. You feel like you are in a movie instead of just watching it.

This movie has a pretty big cast—a bike tour embraces all comers. Even if you've not ridden a bicycle since childhood, you can still have a great time on a bike tour. Perhaps you have pedaled some day trips but want to know more about equipment, planning, or training to improve the quality of your bike touring experience. Or maybe you've done a fondly remembered tour or two but have yet to find time to do more. You may also be an experienced cyclist who wants more information about packing your bike, on-the-roll maintenance, or finding the truly tough and wild two-wheeled adventures.

This book is for anyone who wants that different kind of vacation that combines a love of cycling with travel. You'll benefit from the information in this book if you're riding for the first time or if your bike is gathering dust in the basement (maybe complete with flat tires you haven't the slightest notion how to fix). Or if you ride regularly but just haven't carved out the time—or inspired the right friends and loved ones to go on a bike adventure with you—you can gain from the tips here. You don't have to be planning a cross-country odyssey to use this advice. Some of the skills you'll learn can make you a safer rider on weekend long rides or short trips to the park with your kids. In all cases, this book can be your companion on the road and trails, helping you know the feeling that flows from escaping on a bicycle.

As a compilation of tips from more than 40 years of *Bicycling* magazine, this book pulls together the collective wisdom of hundreds upon hundreds of writers, editors, and readers. This touring information includes loads of time-tested tips and road-proven advice. The knowledge here is what has worked for not just one person but thousands. There's more than one way to ride around the world, and here we've compiled the best insights. For example, the training advice on how to ride 100 miles in a day has helped about a million riders complete century rides.

Because this book is the ultimate how-to guide, it's not going to be filled with other riders' travel adventure stories. Instead, you'll learn how you can create your own amazing memories on a bike.

Go, enjoy. Ride.

CHAPTER 1

How to Pick the Right Trip for You

What to expect during your next cycling vacation

With apologies to Forrest Gump, taking a bike tour is like a box of chocolates. It's an extravagantly delicious escape from reality. Like candy melting in your mouth, your worries dissolve as you pedal mile after mile after mile. With the amazing varieties available in every corner of the world, there's a favorite flavor for everyone. Yet tours also have the same downside as that box of bonbons: If you don't know what you're biting off, you may be in for a nasty surprise. And halfway through, you can't just put it back in the box.

To sort of poke the bottom of tours to give you a preview of what you're in for, this chapter will explain the different types of cycling vacations. First, to find out which kind of trip is best for you, take the quiz on the following page. Then read on for details about particular types of tours.

If you agree with a statement in the quiz, place a check mark in all of the circles in that row. After responding to all the statements along the left side of the quiz, look for the columns with the most checked circles. Those are the touring options that are right for you.

(continued on page 6)

WHICH TOUR IS YOURS?

Destination (choose all that apply)

	1	2	3	4	5	6	7
You want to stay close to home.						○	
You want to see the country, but you have only 2 weeks' vacation every year.							
Easy Rider is your favorite movie.							
You like to experience other cultures.							
You just need to get away—wherever your pedals can take you.							

Companions: whom you want to ride with (choose all that apply)

	1	2	3	4	5	6	7
You feel comfortable riding in large groups.	○				○		
Skip Disney World; the family's taking a ride.	○	○		○	○		
It's time to escape the rat race.			○	○		○	
You want to get even closer to your spouse.	○	○		○	○	○	
No guys, please.							
You're looking for that special someone who shares your interests.							

Planning: the logistics of getting there and back (choose all that apply)

	1	2	3	4	5	6	7
You're a control freak.		○	○				
You want a no-worry vacation.	○					○	
You hate packing, and you always forget something.	○					○	

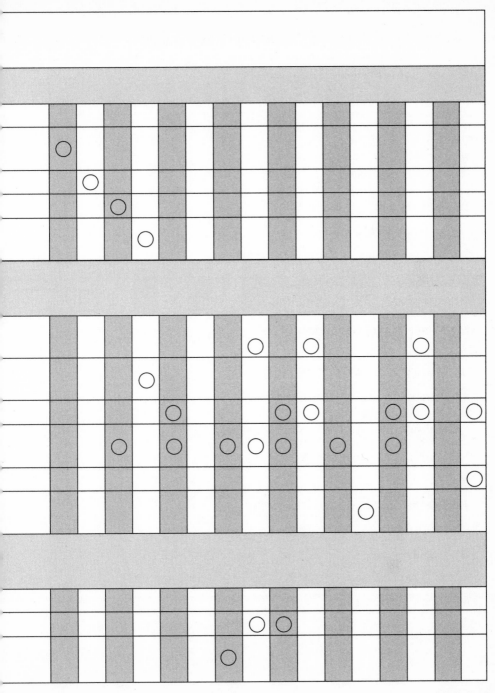

(continued)

WHICH TOUR IS YOURS?—*CONTINUED*

	Supported Group	Do-It-Yourself	Solo	Tandem	Family	Weekender
Lodging: where to stay (choose one)						
Room service is a must.	◯					
You don't mind being tucked in under the stars.		◯				
Money: vacation budgeting (choose all that apply)						
Heat up the plastic—it's splurge time.	◯	◯				
Make it as cheap as possible, please.		◯	◯		◯	
You'll cut corners just to see amazing places.		◯	◯			
Difficulty: relaxing vs. challenging (choose one)						
You already ride at least 75 miles a week.		◯	◯			
You want to bump up your fitness level while on vacation.						
Forget training—this is supposed to be fun.	◯				◯	◯
Special Interest: specialty tours for you						
You're looking for female bonding.						
You want to try a new sport.						
You want help finding a date.						
You want an extreme survival challenge.						
Bring out the vino!						
Welcome race fans!						
You wanna save the world.						

The Right Tour for You Is . . .

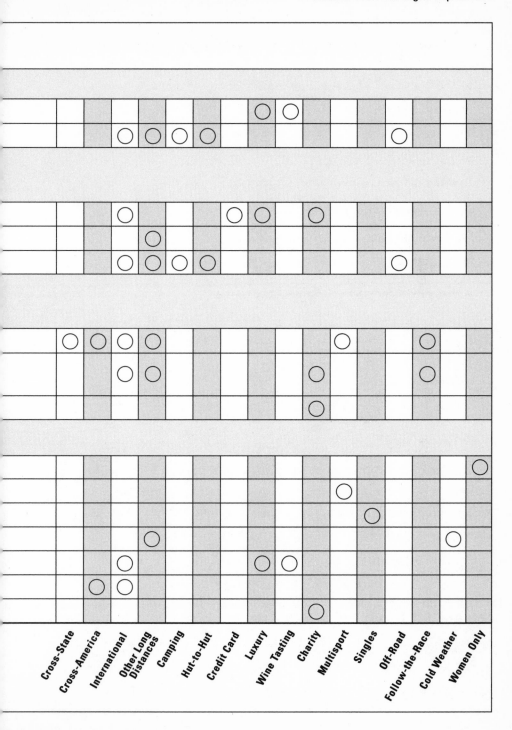

YOUR FIRST DECISION: WHERE?

When picking a tour, your first consideration will probably be location. Of course, it should be someplace that appeals to you. Before you book passage, though, answer these questions.

• What's the best riding season there?

• How will the climate affect your riding?

• What will the terrain be like?

• What kind of physical condition is required to enjoy the ride?

• Will you start and end the tour in the same place?

• How do you get to your starting location?

• How much time will it take to ride where you want to ride?

• Do you speak the language?

• What are the accommodation choices?

The tour you eventually decide upon will probably fall into several of the categories in the quiz, all of which are detailed below. For instance, you and a partner could take a do-it-yourself wine-tasting tour on a tandem. (Hopefully, the rider who sips the most vino won't be steering.) Another example of how tours overlap: a multisport singles tour.

TOUR DETAILS

Supported Group

If you're new to cycling or you haven't been on a tour before, a supported group tour is probably your best bet. The tour company manages everything during the trip, providing well-maintained bikes, planning daily routes that steer you toward off-the-beaten-path attractions, and selecting good places to eat and sleep. Some companies use knowledgeable guide riders to help navigate the route and offer a gentle push up any steep hills. Supported tours also often offer vans, called sag wagons, that will pick you up if you get tired or the weather turns sour. Obviously, you'll pay more (up to about five grand in some cases) for such tours because of all the amenities. More minimalist supported tours simply offer rest stops, support stations, and lodging over a planned route, without including meals and specific attractions.

Because these tours are with groups of riders, often with a range of cycling fitness and skills, you'll probably have to stick with group plans and itineraries. But you'll meet new people and possibly make friends you'll stay in contact with for years. For more information about selecting a touring company, turn to chapter 2.

QUESTIONS TO ASK ANYONE ON TOUR WITH YOU

When you're riding with others (be they significant others or new friends on a group tour), these questions will help manage expectations.

1. How competitive are you? Do you feel like you need to finish first?

2. Do you like to stop often to take pictures, or would you rather continue riding?

3. What's your fitness level? How often do you ride?

4. How flexible are you? Do you need to stick to daily plans?

5. Are you comfortable riding in groups? Do you know how to draft?

Do-It-Yourself

With these tours, you have total freedom and flexibility, but all the planning is on you and any touring companions. You will have to figure out your own routes—often over roads that you don't know; make sleeping arrangements (who knew the Shriners would be in town and book all the rooms?); and, when you're out in the middle of nowhere with nary a cell-phone tower to be seen, rely on yourself to fix any mechanicals to get rolling again. Planning your own tour will let you see some amazing places, often more cheaply than supported tours would. Probably the best thing about do-it-yourself tours is that you'll achieve a sense of independence like you've never felt before, and you can't put a price tag on the can-do feeling you'll have once you finish. For more information about planning your own tour, see chapter 3.

Solo

Take off alone, and you can find yourself as you discover adventure. Free from the schedules of group travel, you make your own way every day. This kind of touring is the ultimate exercise in self-reliance, and you'll need to do more preride planning than for any other kind of trip. You'll also need more equipment, because you'll be packing your home in your panniers. Riding alone doesn't mean you'll be lonely. A loaded bike is a great conversation starter, and you'll likely make lots of friends along the way.

Tandem

One of the biggest advantages of touring tandem is that you don't have to worry about different skill levels forcing one partner to hold back while the other struggles to keep pace. One rider can make up for the other, and together you can go even faster than otherwise. The pilot is responsible for steering and braking; the stoker, in the back, provides additional pedal power. Some tandem bikes are set up to allow the stoker to brake and shift, but often the stoker would rather just take in

SHOULD YOU RIDE A TANDEM WITH YOUR SIGNIFICANT OTHER?

Answer yes to three or more questions below and a tandem may be in your future. Answer no to three or more questions and you should ride separate bikes so your relationship will have a future.

1. Is your partner a novice or a reluctant rider whom you had to coax into the sport?   Yes   No

2. Do you share chores such as washing dishes?   Yes   No

3. When driving in a car together, do you each keep quiet about the other's driving?   Yes   No

4. Do you have a similar pace when riding separate bikes?   Yes   No

5. Does one of you have a poor sense of direction?   Yes   No

the scenery. One disadvantage: You're always together, which means you don't necessarily have the freedom to stop whenever you want, and you have to communicate otherwise automatic functions such as braking. Tandem bikes can cost a couple of thousand dollars, so if you've never ridden one before, try a rental to be sure you both like it.

Family

Several touring companies offer family packages where children ride with parents or are babysat while Mom and Dad ride. With trailers or attachments that allow a child to pedal along while attached to a parent's bike, kids can easily ride along on just about any kind of tour. Once children hit their teens, they're probably strong enough to pedal on their own two wheels. When parents choose the babysitting option,

FIVE QUESTIONS TO ASK
BEFORE TAKING KIDS
ON A SUPPORTED TOUR

1. Is the company insured for child care? You want the option of a tour guide being able to take your child in the van while you ride. Insurance is no guarantee, but at least you'll know the company takes the issue seriously.

2. What babysitting services are available, and how many people watch the children? Make sure babysitting doesn't mean hidden costs; some companies tack it on or offer it on an as-available basis.

3. Are there other kids? You'll want to know if your child will have playmates or if you'll need to keep the little one occupied.

4. What attractions and stops appeal to kids? Playgrounds and beaches are especially good for allowing unstructured time for children to burn off extra energy.

5. What kind of child-related cycling equipment is available? Ask the tour company whether it offers trailers, child seats, or trail-a-bikes. Ideally, you'll have already ridden with your child on the same kind of equipment so both of you know what to expect while rolling.

their kids generally stay and play at a central location to which the adult cyclists circle back at the end of the day's ride.

Weekender

Over the course of a weekend, you can dab your toe into the world of touring. This can let you discover what you like and don't like, helping you to better plan longer trips. A good do-it-yourself weekend plan: Drive a few hours from your home, set up a camp or establish a hotel as a base, and ride a loop from there. In addition to arranging your own meals and lodging, you'll have to find maps and select routes. Some organized weekend tours are century rides that are broken into about 50 miles each day. One downside: You may not get enough—you'll be ready for more, but it'll be time to head back home.

Cross-State

Just about every state has a ride that crosses its expanse from top to bottom or side to side—and some states have both types, often scheduled at different times of the year so cyclists can do both. Some cyclists ride a cross-state like a race, others like a carnival. Some even notch state rides the way some climbers scale the highest peak in every state. The granddaddy of all cross-state tours is Iowa's RAGBRAI (Register's Annual Great Bicycle Race Across Iowa). Started in 1973, the ride covers about 470 miles in a week. For a complete listing of cross-state tours, see Resources on page 214.

Cross-America

In the 1970s, crossing the country by bike was the great American cycling dream. It's nice to know some dreams don't change. There have evolved three ways to head cross-country.

1. An easy, meandering ride when you have many months to discover the country as you span its 3,000-plus miles

2. A course along well-established routes for a bit more of a planned vacation that will take about a month and a half—as long as you don't stop too much

3. A race for cyclists who, like the participants in the Race Across America (RAAM), actually enjoy 5 days of a sleepless, coast-to-coast blur

International

When you travel through another country on a bike, you not only see other places but immerse yourself in their cultures, traditions, and cuisines. You'll meet people off the common tourist routes, and they'll likely welcome you, since many places around the world are more respectful of cyclists than the United States is. Drivers often expect to see cyclists, and trains and other public transportation are bike-friendly. Accommodations are a bit different from domestic travel: You can often hop from B-and-B to B-and-B for reasonable rates. With international guided cycling tours, you'll usually get the most bang for your buck by taking longer vacations of between 10 days and 2 weeks.

Other Long Distances

A good way to take an out-there, self-guided trip is to rent a van with some buddies. While one person drives the van, the others cycle. Everyone takes turns driving over the course of a week or two. You can keep costs low by camping, or you can pull into hotels at night. Greedy rider tip: Look ahead on your route schedule so you're not stuck driving the van on the best day for riding.

Camping

The nightly ceiling of stars may be the romantic justification for taking such a tour, but there's another, more practical reason to camp out. Whether you're on a mountain bike tour in the Outback or a road tour that connects campgrounds, snoozing in a sleeping bag can save you big bucks. On both supported and do-it-yourself tours, you can save about two-thirds by pitching a tent instead of staying in hotels. Whenever possible, though, ask permission before setting up on a stranger's land. And for such renegade camping, avoid large, bright tents.

Hut-to-Hut

Popular in the northwest United States and some places in Europe, the routes of these off-road tours link small, usually primitive cabins where you spend the nights. When you sign up with a tour company, the huts will be stocked with food, cooking equipment, eating utensils, beds, and blankets. This is good, because you can travel through the wilderness without a load of equipment. If you plan a hut-to-hut trip yourself, you'll have to pack along more, though. Another variation of these trips is the guidepost tour, which leads you on a trailless route across open plains by connecting guideposts. Hut-to-hut is actually a misnomer for most of these kinds of tours, because often you camp under the stars. Some, though, do have crude cabins along the way.

Credit Card

Ah, the freedom—you, your bike, and a little piece of plastic. GPS devices and cell phones have made credit-card traveling even easier by allowing you to get directions and call ahead to scout dining and lodgings on the fly. You can also stop in at libraries, borrow a computer, and Priceline.com your way around the countryside. However, free isn't always so free. Because you're not hauling sleeping bags and tents, you'll have to do more pretrip planning and stick to a route that's fairly close to civilization. Along with that plastic, you'll still need to pack a change of clothes and a few other essentials such as tools and rain gear. Finally, a financial fair warning: You'll probably spend more than you expect, because you'll rely on others and facilities on the road when you have changes in plans or emergencies.

Luxury

Even if you don't live the high life every day, luxury tours can give it to you for a little while. Between rides, you can be pampered in some of the plushest lodgings in the world. Do you ride hard enough to deserve the comfort? Who cares? These are no-worry trips. Operators of such tours provide high-end amenities such as wine and food tastings and hot showers ready right after rides. Ride on this kind of tour, and you'll know the operators take pains to ensure that the only things you need to think about are your next pedal stroke and what to order for the dessert course. Expect to pay about three grand or more for such a tour—but what a trip.

Wine Tasting

As the Italians are fond of saying: In wine, truth. On these trips, the truth is that it's hard to tell which is more enjoyable—the riding or the vino. The most famous places for such tours are California's beautiful Sonoma and Napa Valleys, France, and Italy. Routes are planned between wineries, where wine experts can educate your tastebuds, and cycling experts can help you with routes.

Charity

You double your pleasure on charity rides because you catch a beautiful ride while raising money for a good cause with lots of other likeminded cyclists. Some charity rides require that you donate a set amount to participate; others ask you to collect pledges for each mile you pedal. The pace of a charity tour is usually relaxed, and part of the fun is enjoying the company of others who support the same cause. You'll likely see lots of other riders and many first-time touring cyclists on such tours. One of the best-attended and best-known charity rides is Lance Armstrong's Ride for the Roses, benefiting the Lance Armstrong Foundation.

Multisport

These tours combine cycling with other types of physical activities. There are lots of varieties of tours, including kayak/bike, hike/bike, ski/bike, surf/bike, snowshoe/bike, and climb/bike. These trips are ideal if you are good at one sport and your traveling companion is good at another. You'll each have exposure to the other's sport in a relaxing environment. Stick with touring companies that have been offering such packages for 4 or 5 years; they have experience riding and planning routes, and will most likely have a rapport with the local hotels and restaurants.

Singles

Everyone on these trips has one thing on their minds: cycling. Okay, okay, perhaps they're also thinking about meeting other singles who enjoy riding. Ask the tour operator about the average age and the male-female ratio before plunking down your deposit. And if a fellow rider repeatedly drops you on the climbs, he or she is not interested.

Off-Road

These tours start where the pavement ends. As with on-road tours, you can choose fully supported tours that offer gourmet cuisine and massages, or you can load yourself up and be self-sufficient. Off-road supported group tours are usually smaller than their asphalt-borne cousins, with many touring groups limited to about 15 people. For self-planned or solo off-road adventures, you'll have to plot routes to ensure that you don't get lost, you know the terrain, and you can handle anything Mother Nature throws your way. See chapter 6 for lots of specific info about mountain bike touring.

FIVE WAYS TO HOOK UP ON A SINGLES TOUR

1. Don't ride fast to "impress."

2. Keep your paws to yourself.

3. Bathe daily. Yes, especially there.

4. Don't be shy; strike up a conversation early in the tour.

5. Make sure that the conversation starter isn't a cheesy line like "Is that a banana in your jersey pocket, or are you just happy to see me?"

Follow-the-Race

Along the Champs-Elysées, the crowd cheers so loud you can't hear yourself grin. What's even more unbelievable is that they cheer for *you*. Even if you haven't broken into the ranks of the elite pro riders, several tour companies offer an experience identical to many famous cycling races such as the Tour de France, Giro d'Italia, and Paris-Roubaix. These tours allow riders to precede or follow the racers along the route. In addition to letting you ride the same roads and tell your friends just how tough Alpe d'Huez is, these tours also allow plenty of time to watch the race. You can do self-supported versions, but tour guides and companies often have know-how about navigating around traffic congestion and insider info for slipping into postrace parties.

Cold Weather

If you enjoy the challenge of pitting yourself against nature, a cold-weather tour may be for you. Mistakes that you can get away with in summer can lead to frostbite or worse during harsh winter rides. On such tours, you need to allow extra time to negotiate bad weather and let your body adapt to the conditions and recover. One of the benefits: You'll enjoy nearly deserted roads (especially since few tour companies run such trips, so you'll probably be on your own) and have a better view along the way.

Women Only

Testosterone need not apply. Some tour companies specialize in women-only tours, and larger companies will often have women-only groups on their regular routes, on and off road and to a variety of destinations. Some of the things women like about these female-only excursions: no competitiveness; no worries about being hit on; and a friendly, supportive environment along the way. Also, many make friends and find riding partners for when they return back home.

CHAPTER 2

How to Pick

a Tour Company

When others do the planning, you just need to worry about the pedaling—and the payments

Bike tour company operators are sort of like air traffic controllers. They have lots of things in the air at one time: securing lodging, making sure meals are served on time, and herding a group of riders from day to day. By signing up for a tour through a company, you don't have to worry about these potential logistical nightmares. The trade-off: money and, of course, finding the right company.

Some tour companies simply provide route maps and suggestions on where to stay, and you have contact with those companies only through the mail. The majority, however, offer guided, or supported, tours. These trips are great if you're a novice bike tourist. In addition to providing information about the locale you're riding through, guides can also offer valuable cycling advice to help you ride better. Guides with mechanical know-how are on hand to fix your bike, if needed. Such tours are a good choice if you lack the time or inclination to do trip planning. Instead of having to haul out maps and figure out ways around high-traffic roads, you can rely on a touring company to thoroughly scout routes. A supported tour is also a good choice if you're looking for an experience that's closer to a vacation than a by-the-seat-of-your-pants adventure. And with so many companies and trips available these days, it's easy to find a commercial trip with a destination and level of difficulty that suits your individual skills, fitness, and ambition.

As fun as riding a bike for a living may sound, you should remember that for tour operators, it's a business. Knowing some of the ins and outs of how they operate will allow you to better choose a tour you'll be happy with. Some of the things you should consider include how much your deposit will be and whether you should buy trip insurance. Among the other, more fun things to decide is where you'll go and what kind of side attractions you'll see. This chapter will help you find the company that best suits your needs.

COMPANY FINDER CHECKLIST

Destination. This is likely your first consideration. Be sure the place appeals to you, and do some research about the locale. Look for sources outside of the tour company's Web site and brochures. Good references include chambers of commerce and bike shops. Along with attractions and scenery, you should think about what the terrain will be like and whether the riding will be hilly or flat. For international destinations, it's a good idea to check the U.S. State Department's Web site, www.state.gov, to see if there are any security concerns in the country you're heading to.

While some companies offer all-inclusive tours that include airfare or other initial transportation arrangements, often you're responsible for getting to the tour's start point (and getting back home again from its end point) on your own. This is definitely something to consider when pricing a trip.

Timing. Do you want to see spring blossoms or fall foliage on your ride? Also consider climate: Can you handle desert heat in July, or would you rather wait for cooler October weather before heading to Moab? Figure out when you'd like to take your trip, and contact the tour company at least 3 months before departure. Popular tours book fast, so you may even need to book 6 months ahead of time.

10 QUESTIONS TO ASK A TOUR COMPANY

1. What are the lodgings?

2. What's the average daily mileage?

3. How hard is the terrain?

4. What does the support consist of?

5. How much baggage is allowed?

6. What kinds of bikes are offered?

7. How long have you been in business?

8. Are your guides locals?

9. How much is the deposit?

10. How many meals are included per day?

Touring companies set their schedules in the winter, so the best time to start scouting for a trip is late December or after the first of the year. By then, the companies will have updated their Web sites and brochures. That's also when it's good to scout ads in magazines such as *Outside, Travel & Leisure, Bike, Bicycling,* and *Mountain Bike.*

Price. Supported tours can be costly, with higher-end, longer trips topping $4,000. However, you can find some for less than a grand. There's a pretty uniform equation for tour pricing: The lower the cost, the more you should expect to do yourself. A less expensive tour may not have a dedicated support vehicle to pick up tired riders. Meals are another thing to go when the price of a tour drops. On a cheaper tour, you'll often be on your own for most, if not all, food. Also, when prices are lower—under $1,000—you'll probably be roughing it by camping or staying in lower-end lodgings, such as chain hotels, instead of the bed-and-breakfasts and luxury suites of the higher-end tours.

Another thing to look at when considering the cost of a tour is the price per day. Often, trips longer than 10 days offer good value because the price per day is lower. Unlike discount airlines and hotels, touring companies offer few last-minute deals. They're run on a fairly tight margin and they don't overbook. However, you may get a discount if you get a group of friends (10 to 14 riders) to commit to a tour. Even if the company can't schedule a trip exclusively for your group, you can merge with a scheduled trip. This allows for smaller groups and more flexibility for later sign-ups.

Other riders. When picking a tour, think about whom you'll be riding with. In addition to the time on the bike, you'll likely be hanging out with these people during dinners and maybe even sharing lodging. The tour company will be able to offer general demographics of who takes which tours. For example, some tours might attract more singles, while others draw families. Also, it's acceptable to ask for general information about people who've already signed up for a tour you'd like to take. The company will likely tell you the male-to-female ratio and approximate ages. To scope out whether there will be people who'll ride at the same pace as you, ask if there are riders who have similar fitness levels and skill levels to yours.

And ask about the number of people in your group, so you get a better feel for the interaction you'll have with group leaders. With more people, you'll have to contend with such things as waiting for others and slower transfers from place to place. Smaller groups are more convenient, but you'll miss out on meeting some interesting personalities. Most companies won't take groups of larger than 24. Conversely, if too few people sign up for a specific tour, the company may reschedule or offer a refund.

Whatever the number of people you'll be riding with, you'll have to be prepared to make compromises. You might have to take a side trip because the rest of the group wants to; or perhaps the others will opt for a shorter route one day. However, many touring companies are flexible and allow individual riders to go it on their own for a while, as long as they know where to meet at the end of the day.

The size of the group relates to the tour's price only if you and your buddies are reserving a trip specifically for yourselves. In that case, the tour company may ask for more per head if your group is smaller—say, less than 10. And for this kind of arrangement, to keep your price per head lower, the company may still ask permission to include others not affiliated with your group.

Lodging. Lodging should be a primary consideration. Figure out what you like: luxury hotels or a sky full of stars. Ask the touring company where you'll be staying, and then check out the Web or brochures to see photos of the accommodations. For a tour that'll be staying in hotels, ask the touring company how long they've worked with those hotels. Check out the hotels' Web sites, which may provide you additional information about the locales, too. Be wary of companies that say their lodgings vary frequently; this means they may not have ongoing relationships with local establishments. Worst-case scenario: You show up at the end of a long day of riding to find out you don't have a hotel room. Especially if you're taking your own bike on tour, you might want to ask the tour company about security measures. Find out where the bikes are stored at night (they're usually kept on the support van) and what kind of locks are used.

Cuisine. On some tours, half the reason for going is the food. Many companies offer trips where you ride from haute cuisine to haute cuisine destination. Many also provide on-the-bike snacks along the way, lugged around either by the tour guide or in the support van. Find out how many other meals per day are included in the trip. Are you going to have to find or prepare some food yourself? Is there a preplanned menu? Do you want to taste the flavor of the area you're visiting, or

WHAT IF YOU CANCEL?

You'll have to pay for your trip in full before you leave. Some companies set up installment plans; others ask for a lump sum. Almost all require deposits to protect themselves from casual cancellations. Most contracts will outline the provisions of deposits, and the typical deposit is 15 to 20 percent of the tour cost. Often, the further out you cancel, the more likely you'll be to get some of your money back. You probably won't get the entire deposit back, because that's what is used to reserve your spot and make advance arrangements, such as hotel and restaurant reservations, which are difficult and costly to change.

A typical refund policy offers a full refund, minus the deposit, for any cancellation 60 days or more from the departure date. Within 60 to 30 days of the tour, you can expect 50 to 70 percent of the tour cost or a full or partial credit for a future ride. If you cancel a month to 2 weeks before a trip, you'll be lucky to get a partial credit for a future trip. And if you bail on a tour 2 weeks or less before the scheduled departure, don't figure on getting any money back. You're lucky if a company even gives you a credit within this period.

Especially in today's unpredictable world, buying trip insurance might be a good answer. For a $2,000 trip, insurance costs can vary among companies, from $60 to more than $125. Coverage includes trip cancellation or interruption, missing baggage, and emergency medical expenses and transportation.

would you prefer to stick to food that'll fuel your pedaling? It'll be a terrible experience if every time you belly up to the table you cringe at what's served. This is especially true if you have special dietary considerations: Some companies do accommodate vegetarians, cyclists with diabetes, and people with other nutritional needs.

Guides. Ask about the experience of the guides. If the company already has a guide assigned to your tour, find out if that person has guided in the area before and, if so, for how many years. At least 1 year of guiding is a good measure. Also, if you'll be in another country, it'd be better to have a guide who's from there. That way, you'll learn more about the local people and culture.

Routes. Often, the tour company will have routes and itineraries available ahead of time; some companies may post routes on their Web sites. Almost all say that routes and itineraries are subject to change slightly. Even so, having a general idea of your planned route will allow you to gauge how hard the riding will be and how much time will be allotted for sightseeing and going off to do your own activities. Sometimes side tours cost extra or require adjustments in the daily plan. Find out what kind of support the company will offer if you go off by yourself. For example, the company may be willing to send the support van to pick you up and take you back to the hotel, saving you from riding back. The company may even offer to send a guide along with you to tell you about the sights.

Packing. In the event that you want to travel light, tour companies usually offer a selection of rental bikes, from high-end road bikes to hybrids to tough, full-suspension bikes for off road. The company may also be able to rent you a helmet, if necessary. If you prefer your own saddle and pedals, check to be sure it's okay to have them installed on bikes the company offers. Some will even have them put on a bike and ready for you, if you ship them ahead of time.

Of course, you can always choose to take your own bike. When taking it to the tour start point on a domestic airline flight, expect to pay a shipping fee of anywhere from $40 to $75 each way. With certain airlines, you can get this fee reduced or eliminated by joining a cycling organization such as the League of American Bicyclists (www.bikeleague.org) or the International Mountain Bicycling Association (www.imba.com). On most international trips, you don't have to pay an additional bike-shipping charge. Check out "How to Box Your Bike" on page 40 for instructions on preparing your bike for its flight.

Often, supported tours provide handlebar bags into which you can transfer items such as sunglasses, snacks, a tool kit, a lightweight rain jacket, a hat, and a camera (see "Everything but the Bike" on page 52 for advice on choosing basic cycling equipment). Ask whether the tour requires any special equipment, such as cold-weather clothing (see chapter 9 for info on packing for weather extremes) or extra hydration systems. You should also find out how dressy the nights will be—some hotels and restaurants may be more upscale and require dressier clothes. For a camping or hut-to-hut tour, you'll need to check on what kind of outdoor equipment the tour company will provide; you might be on your own when it comes to cooking food. (If so, see "Camping Adds" on page 35 for guidelines on what to take.)

References. Before you book with a company, find out how long it's been in business. A good minimum: 5 years. Request references from former customers in your area and give them a call. Don't rely on the happy-customer quotes in brochures and Web sites—of course companies are going to publish only good stuff about themselves.

Another important question to ask as you're checking references (especially for international tours) is whether the company uses subcontractors—the people you're writing the check to may not be the ones guiding the tour. For international tours, you should ask if the company has offices based in their destination countries. If they do, that's a good indication that they know the region and can provide a full range of support.

Fine print. Look at the company's agreement. The fine print will have information about cancellations, refund policies, and liability for things such as lost luggage.

See Resources on page 209 for contact information for a variety of specific tour companies.

CHAPTER 3

How to Plan

Your Own Tour

Go anywhere in the world for just about any length of time

The bicycle gets credit for loads of things. For instance, Wilbur and Orville Wright parlayed their bike-repair experience to provide us with airplanes. Some say Einstein had the spark of genius that was the theory of relativity while on a bike ride. The interstate road system was first designed to handle heavy bike traffic. And the bike played an integral part in the women's suffrage movement, providing a mode of transportation away from mundane domestic lives and freeing women from corsets—who could wear one of those while riding?

For women *and* men today, cycling is freedom. And the ultimate touring freedom is following your own route and being your own guide on a trip you plan yourself. Sure, there's lots more planning than simply plunking down some money and showing up at a touring company's door, but the reward is—you guessed it—freedom. You're able to take side trips, linger in doorways while gentle rain passes, and not worry about someone else's schedule. However, the flip side of that freedom is that you have to know enough to support yourself. A little bit of know-how and the right equipment take you a long way on such trips.

This chapter is your guide to sorting through your choices, whether you're going for a weekend ride or a cross-country jaunt. The following information will show you how to plan a route; offer suggestions on what to take, depending on how long you'll be gone; and teach you how to smartly store all your stuff on the bike. You'll also learn how to pack a bike for shipping—an underrated skill that'll keep your bicycle from getting bashed before you even start your trip.

ROUTE PLANNING

Your ride starts at home. Long before your first pedal stroke, you should ride your route on the kitchen table with detailed, accurate, up-to-date maps. While it might seem easy to rip a map out of an atlas and go, you may not get enough or the right kind of information. Because road maps are devoted to automobile travel, you may miss some roads that would be better for cycling.

The best source for planning a cycling route is the touring organization, Adventure Cycling Association (www.adventurecycling.org; 800-755-2453). Two other good sources are the League of American Bicyclists (www.bikeleague.org; 202-822-1333) and the National Bicycle Dealers Association (http://nbda.com; 949-722-6909). Both of these organizations offer useful resources, such as locations of bike shops along your proposed route. Another option for finding accurate maps is to contact the tourism or transportation departments of the areas you'll be riding through.

One thing to always keep an eye on when mapping out a route: elevation. Get a topographical map from state transportation departments as well. By figuring out how much climbing you'll have to do, you'll be better able to plan how far you can go in a day (everyone's slower on climbs). And you can also watch for those eye-popping altitudes above 10,000 feet, where you're likely to feel short of breath and more fatigued if you're not used to the elevation.

Ideally, you should look up information about your destination 3 to

TOP FIVE QUESTIONS TO ANSWER BEFORE YOU GO ON YOUR OWN

1. What's my budget?

2. What's the terrain like?

3. How long do I plan to ride each day?

4. Will I camp or stay in hotels?

5. Where and what am I going to eat?

4 months ahead of time. This will allow plenty of time to hear back from tourism agencies and other sources and to adjust your route and resolve any follow-up questions.

When planning your route, be deliberate. If you're looking for more scenery and your timetable is more relaxed, ride the lesser-traveled roads. Sure, you'd probably like a little built-in wandering, but keep a course and know where you can bail off and catch a major road in an emergency. Before you leave, you should also know whether you'll be camping or playing connect-the-dots with hotel rooms from night to night. If you choose the latter, realize that weather and other potential delays mean you'll need flexibility, so making reservations may not be the best idea. Just call ahead to convention and visitors bureaus to find out whether any special events will be packing hotels. It's good to know if the Southern Baptists will be in town so you can plan another route and stand a chance of getting a room.

For on-the-fly eating, you'll probably find enough restaurants along the way. And more often than you'd think, when you ask locals for recommendations, you'll find yourself sitting down at a new friend's dinner table for a home-cooked meal.

Don't Get Lost

Part of planning your route is knowing what to do in the event that you get lost. Forget the old wives' tales about moss growing on the north side of rocks and clouds always moving from east to west. Clouds travel in different directions depending on wind patterns and altitude. And moss? Pish. It can pop up anywhere; sure, it often grows on north-facing rocks and trees simply because there's less sun and moisture on that side, but that's not enough to rely on when you're trying to get back to civilization.

Here are some tips on what to do if you find yourself all turned around. Start by asking yourself what you remember about where you are. Clear thinking might get you back to someplace you recognize. Then you should:

Listen. Stop riding, stand still, and let your breathing calm. Your ears can help you find beacons such as a car driving on a nearby road or the trickle of a stream.

Find reference points. Going in one direction beats wandering in a circle. Even without a compass, you can use the sun and landmarks such as mountains or distant buildings. You can also use terrain to maintain a direction, such as continuing to go downhill and following merging streams.

Start marking your route. After you're lost, to avoid riding in circles, leave a small, nondestructive trail marker, such as two sticks laid out in an X.

Pack along a GPS. A Global Positioning System uses a network of satellites to provide accurate, worldwide positioning and navigation information. By linking to these satellites with a wireless handheld device, you can find out exactly where you are and how fast and in what direction you're moving. The latest models are becoming more and more lightweight and affordable—you can buy one for $100 to $600. The best time to use such a device is when you're traveling off road or in less developed countries. But don't let it be a substitute for map-reading skills, which means you should know how to . . .

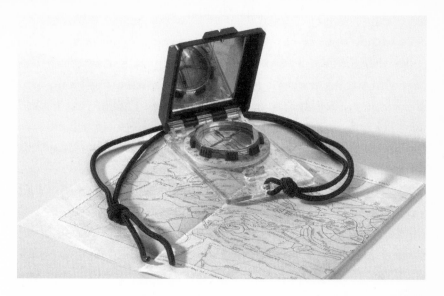

With a few simple map-reading skills, you can navigate your way home—or to just about any other place in the world.

Navigate with a compass. First, find on your map the declination, which is the difference in degrees between true north and magnetic north. Turn the compass dial so that the small, stationary arrow points to the declination degree. Then set your compass on your map. Align the baseplate direction arrow, or the long edge of the compass, with the line indicating true north on the map, and hold the compass in place. Hold the map and compass and rotate them until the magnetic needle's colored end is inside the orienting arrow. The map is now aligned to the land in front of you.

PACKING CHECKLISTS

When deciding what to take on a bike tour, the first question to ask yourself is: What do you really need in order to enjoy yourself? Some touring cyclists roll out the door with only an energy bar and a spare tube. Others have been known to pack such items as camp lanterns, ham radios, portable Global Position Systems, and even hair dryers. Take whatever you want, as long as you're ready to go slower.

So when the time comes to pack for your trip, take it personally. Decide what you need, what to leave behind, and what to buy on the road if necessary. Then, before leaving, take a hard look at your packed items. Do yourself a favor: Eliminate a few things (too much postride clothing is a common mistake). Lightening your load pays dividends for your ride, your peace of mind, and your legs.

One important factor in your packing decisions is what sort of tour you will take. You'll require increasing amounts of gear depending on whether you are going on a weekend tour, weeklong ride, cross-country journey, or international tour. And obviously you'll want to dress for the weather. Chapter 9 provides details about the specific stuff you should take for weather extremes.

Another point is your own personal quotient for creature comforts. You may prefer, say, more than one pair of sunglasses or a special tube of hair gel, while others just don't want to skimp on camera equipment.

LOCK 'EM UP

Sometimes you have to be away from your bike. Carry a U-lock, but with a group, a longer chain with a combination lock works better to lock several bikes together without carrying a bunch of heavy locks. Also check into whether ranger stations will store your bike overnight.

When camping, some people put tent stakes through the bike frame. Lay the bike down and run tent poles through the front and back wheels. If someone tries to steal the bike, they'll bring down the tent. You can also remove the front wheel and seatpost, take them into the tent with you, and then stake down the frame.

Again, take it personally. But here is a baseline guide to what you should take on a self-supported tour in addition to your usual helmet, shorts, gloves, jersey, and shoes.

Weekend Tour

A basic setup for a weekend tour can serve as your foundation for longer, more ambitious trips. The bags you pack will include a handlebar bag, rear pannier (one side only), and equipment that can be installed or mounted on the bike itself. Here's the breakdown.

Handlebar Bag

This becomes most everyone's favorite stash. It is your place on the bike where many convenient items are in reach, so you don't have to stop the bike or even lose much pace.

A quality bag may cost as much as $100. Look for a brand with lots of easy-access pockets and zippers. The items in your handlebar bag will vary, but you should keep them light and limited to the things that you need to keep within reach, including:

Sunglasses. Make sure your eyes are covered, for ultraviolet-ray protection.

Sun/rain hat. Preferably, pack one that has a back flap to cover your neck, along with a sufficient bill for water protection.

Headlamp. For about $25, you can have an extra, highly efficient light in your bag for any occasion. You might have to ride farther than anticipated at dusk. Wilderness does come with sudden weather shifts. Or you might need some extra illumination when setting up camp. A headlamp-style light keeps your hands free so you can work faster before it gets completely dark.

Multiuse pocketknife. A good example is a Swiss Army Classic. The more options, the better. Such a knife is a wonderful backup maintenance kit for your bike.

First-aid kit. You can buy a prepacked kit for less than $10. Or here's a do-it-yourself kit: antiseptic wipes, 12 sizes of adhesive bandages, gauze pads, antibiotic cream, medical tape (or duct tape, which can also be used for other repairs), pain relievers, Bag Balm (for chafing), Pepto-Bismol or a comparable digestive soother, a bee-sting kit (if you're allergic to bees), tweezers, a needle and thread, and some form of first-aid literature.

Camera. A conveniently sized automatic-focus and perhaps water-resistant camera is good for spontaneity. Of course, you won't be snapping and pedaling at the same time, but seconds count when you want the perfect photo.

Journal. Keep a small notebook and pen handy, and you will be thrilled at the notes you'll have to read once you're back home. There's also therapy in the writing itself.

Map. Have a map with details about your route, especially if you are planning to improvise along the way. But don't pack whole map books or three maps of the same route.

LAST-MINUTE TRIP CHECKLIST

Sometimes you just want to go out and ride. Here is a spur-of-the moment trip checklist.

- Bike (duh)
- Helmet
- Gloves
- Water
- Seatbag-style repair kit with multitool
- Camera
- Tarp, which can serve as a tent
- Sleeping bag, strapped onto a rack
- Pullover fleece or rain jacket, also on the rack
- Credit card

Backup don't-get-lost device. Take a compass or a GPS in case the map is not enough to keep you on track.

Pepper spray. One of the greatest concerns, especially for solo cyclists, is safety. Carrying pepper spray can give you a sense of security, but some states have laws that regulate the spray's potency. (And on trips outside the United States, forget it. In addition to the problem of getting pepper spray past airline security, it is illegal in some countries and can get your Lycra-covered butt thrown in jail.)

Cell phone. Always helpful in case of emergency.

On-the-bike snacks. Be sure to put some finger foods in your handlebar bag for easy noshing. See chapter 8 for details about the types of munchies that are best to eat while in the saddle.

Rear Pannier

For a weekend trip, you should need only one side pannier. You can buy one for less than $200 that'll fit loads of gear without adding too much weight. Look for one made with weatherproof material such as Gore-Tex, in case you encounter wet weather. Here's the rear pannier checklist.

Rain jacket and pants. There is no skimping here, even if you are a professional meteorologist who sees no rain in the forecast. Nothing wrecks a trip more quickly than getting drenched—and nothing adds to the possible adventure more than having a terrific ride despite the elements. Gore-Tex is still the gold standard. You might pay up to $300 for the jacket and pants, but you will thank yourself in a downpour.

Extra shirt. Not two or three extra, just one.

Socks. A hugely underestimated joy is putting on a clean, dry pair of socks at day's end.

Extra bike shorts. Stink means bacteria. Swapping shorts keeps you fresh down there.

Hygiene kit. Include sunscreen, soap, razor, toothpaste, toothbrush, deodorant, and towel.

Repair and tool kit. A minimal kit should have lube, duct tape, patch kits, a spare tube (dust your replacement tube with talcum powder for easier handling), and a multitool with a chain breaker. When wrapping tools and other metal items, use a small towel to buffer any rattling. Binding the goods with rubber bands keeps everything compact and quiet. See chapter 10 for additional details about the tools you should take on tour.

On the Bike

Some of your essential items for your weekend tour can be fitted right on the bike by adding a rear-wheel rack that lets you bungee items to the top. You can buy a sturdy one for about $60, but don't put on too much weight here. Some are very easy to install, clipping onto the seatpost with a quick-release similar to the ones on your wheels. The following items can also be carried on your bike, using their own mounts.

Water bottle and cage. As automatically as you wear a helmet, you should install as many water bottle cages as your frame can support. It's always nice to have the option of throwing on more water instead of shriveling up in the Arizona sun.

Pump. Get one that fits inside your frame and can easily pump up to the pressure in your tires. (Some pumps can't handle the higher pressure of road tires.) A full-frame pump, which is longer than the micro pumps often used by mountain bikers, will make the job of changing a flat faster, because you won't have to pump as much. Another option that's easy to stow in a seat pack is a CO_2 pump. You should probably pack at least two extra cartridges, though.

Lock. Buy one with a combination, so you don't have to worry about losing a key. Nothing is worse than having your bike locked up when the key is no place to be found.

Mirror. If you don't feel comfortable sneaking peeks over your shoulder, this rearview device costs less than $20 but comes in handy on busy roads.

Camping Adds

Remember, when camping, leave no trace. What you pack in, pack out. And if you are planning to camp, here are other suggestions for the pannier.

Cookware and spoon. You can find a 2-liter titanium pot with a spoon to make your suppers easier and tastier. The price is under $100—you can spend that in one day of restaurant meals on the road.

Camp stove. Where there's cookware, there needs to be heat. A lightweight yet effective model should cost about $70.

Food. Your selection will be by trial and error, but this per-person grocery list is a good base: 8 to 16 ounces of rice, 8 ounces of pasta, four to six energy bars, packets of herbs and spices, four jerky packets (beef, turkey, salmon, and veggies), two hot chocolate packets, and one or two freeze-dried camp meals as backup. Supplement this basic supply with restaurant meals or impromptu grocery stops for raw veggies, fruit, fig bars, and other favorite foods to add variety to your meals.

When you'll be sleeping under the stars, strap the following equipment onto the bike itself, on a rear rack.

Sleeping bag. Roll it up tight and strap it lengthwise onto the top of the rear rack. Remember, bulky is not good. Neither is old, musty, or ripped. If you are serious about becoming a weekend tourer, a good sleeping bag is more than worth the $200 investment. Look for one that is warm, durable, and able to be tightly rolled. If you're not sure that camp touring is for you, a sleeping bag is still likely to come in handy on other outdoor occasions.

Sleeping pad. This is an underrated item that provides lots of comfort for little space and money. You can get a good one for less than $20. Roll it up with the sleeping bag to save space.

DID YOU PACK TOO MUCH?

Answering no to any of the first four questions or yes to the final two means it's time to repack.

1. Can you lift your bike and carry it 100 yards? It may be necessary to do just that on wilderness tours where the road runs out or a river must be crossed. Or you might simply need to bypass a construction zone. In any case, if you can't lift the bike, you've loaded too much gear onto it.

2. Are you carrying more than 40 pounds? Be a weight geek: Break out a scale to see how much you're packing. If you're carrying more than 40 pounds, including all your bags and equipment, you've got too much stuff.

3. Have you eliminated one item for every five you're taking? The true minimalists (and generally less-weighted-down cyclists) will shoot for much lower ratios.

4. Can you lift your bike over a fence? Not to go pool-hopping—this might help you take a significant shortcut. If you can't lift the bike, see the details after question 1.

5. At the end of your last tour, were you carrying any items you hadn't used? If so, eliminate 'em this time.

6. Are you constantly thinking about how heavy your bike is? This is a simple—yet critical—question for your tour. Make it your mission to answer no.

Nylon tarp and rope. For weekend camping, a strung-up tarp is just as effective as a tent, without all of that extra weight. Take 12 to 16 feet of climbing rope.

Weeklong Tour

The extra 4 to 5 days means it's time for a second rear pannier. You can balance out the load with these items.

Extra jersey. Getting by with one jersey is possible, but a second one doesn't add much weight and has the distinct advantage of providing comfort for you and perhaps your riding mates.

Two more pairs of socks and underwear. You may still need to wash out some items, though the quantities here are enough for many cyclists.

Another pair of bike shorts. In fact, if you're a woman, you might want to pack a clean pair of shorts for each day of your trip. Oh, this is not excessive. Your butt (and sensitive female areas in that vicinity) will thank you.

A good book. Stick with a paperback and make it one you truly will read.

Five extra spokes. This is the number suggested by veteran cyclists.

Spare cable. Look for the kind that will serve as either brake or derailleur cable so you don't have to carry as many. Ask your bike shop wrench to show you how to replace broken cable.

Extra tube. Every extra flat-fixer is only about $5 and well worth the extra ounces.

Address book. It's great to be able to send postcards to friends and loved ones. However, you're defeating the purpose of a tour if you take your PDA and work by wi-fi.

Extra water bottles or a hydration system. You'll need lots more water, and you may not have the convenience of rest stops every 20 miles. Add another water bottle (or two), or if you prefer, strap a hydration pack on your back. For hot tours, you can pack an extra bladder and have it ready to swap.

Camping Adds

If you are camping instead of sleeping above ground (in a bed-and-breakfast, hotel, hostel, or other lodging), here are other items you should include.

Campsite shorts. It'll be a long week. Changing into "normal" clothes will feel amazingly refreshing.

Double food. Take along about twice the amount that you would for a weekend tour. Use restaurants to break up your routine and save on load.

Sandals. Another creature comfort for campers.

Polypropylene top and bottom. A big plus on colder days and nights. The high-end stuff can be pricey—as much as $300—but you can find some that'll keep you dry for $70 to $80.

Light tent. You don't need a multiseason, heavier tent for most weeklong rides. You should be able to find a good, durable model for less than $200.

Cross-Country Tour

The added gear for this ambitious and admirable form of touring is about time savings and heightened readiness for the ride. Here's the add-on list, which can be accommodated, in part, with a seatbag that you can buy for $15 to $25.

Waterproof oversocks. This $40-plus item will help protect against cold, rain, and dampness.

Insulated, waterproof gloves. There is considerable debate about the necessity or purity of wearing cycling gloves, but no one downplays the value of outer-shell gloves on colder days. About $70 will save your fingers hours of misery.

Fleece pullover. You probably have one in your closet. If not, buy one with a hood. It'll be a good middle-insulation layer.

Extra tire. Not just a tube but a tire.

More water. If you haven't already added a third water bottle, time to belly up.

Bungee cords. Loads of unforeseen uses for these puppies may come up as you ride coast-to-coast—from strapping on souvenirs to creating a stretchy bike security system using tree branches.

Extra batteries for headlamp. Some cyclists recommend taking this precaution even on weeklong trips.

Stamps. Don't promise you'll find a post office along the way.

Swimsuit. For an impromptu romp through the town fountain or, better yet, a dip in a pristine lake or flowing river.

Camping Adds

Water treatment tablets. Easy to carry and inexpensive, at about $8. By trip's end, these will have been either untouched or an undeniable ride saver.

Multiseason tent. Go the extra $50 to $100 for a tent that will hold up to the weather. Buy one only as big as the number of bodies you anticipate accommodating.

Emergency blanket. Find one that's good quality, with insulation, yet thin. Ten bucks at most outdoor stores will fill the bill.

International Adventure

On these types of tours, if you don't have the equipment to match your ambition, you could end up stuck in the middle of nowhere for a long, long time. Here are some additional items that can be stowed in two front panniers.

Two more extra T-shirts. Not three, four, or five. Think utility (and perhaps the politics of the region) when choosing colors and tops with logos or designs.

Insulated cold-weather tights.

Hiking boots. Go for a light, midankle model to save on weight.

Long pants. Heck, you might be invited to a fancy sit-down dinner. This isn't the 1980s, so don't choose a baggy pair.

Dress shirt. You will be in a better-attired position to accept that dinner invitation.

Second extra tire.

Spare brake.

Up to 10 feet of brake/derailleur cable.

Two more extra tubes.

Water system. Add either a collapsible water container or a water

(continued on page 42)

HOW TO BOX YOUR BIKE

Without a touring company to provide you a ride, and because you want to take your trusty wheels with you, you need to know how to pack your bike to ship it when you have to take a plane, train, or bus to your tour departure point. Here are the steps to ensure your bike will arrive safely and ready to roll.

1. Find a box. The quickest, easiest way is to ask for one at your local bike shop. Get one that's big enough for your bike and a smaller parts box that'll fit inside the large box. The other option is to buy a specially designed bike crate with foam padding and straps to secure your bike. It'll cost $100 to $300, but it allows easy access and prevents jostling.

2. Remove the seatpost. By either loosening the seatpost quick-release or binder bolt with a hex wrench, slide out the seatpost. Keep the seat attached and place the whole thing in the parts box.

3. Slide off the handlebar. Slacken the cables so you can remove the bar without completely disconnecting the brake and shifter cables. For a more modern, nonthreaded stem, simply remove the faceplate with a hex wrench to take off the bar. For a threaded stem, loosen the wedge bolt at the top of the stem to twist the whole stem from the head tube. For brake cables, undo the releases on the brake arms or levers. Then remove the cables and housings from the stops on the frame. Create slack in the shifter cables by clicking and pedaling into the biggest-cog/big-chainring combination, then shifting up for the rear and down for the front without pedaling. If the front derailleur kicks off the chain even though you didn't pedal, try again, this time holding the derailleur by hand. Remove the housing from the stops.

4. Remove the pedals. Right pedal counterclockwise, left clockwise. Remember the rule: Spin back for off, forward for on. Pack them in the parts box.

5. Stow other accessories in the parts box. Pack the bike com-

puter and any other loose parts you've attached to your bike. Remove the quick-release and pack it, too. Add your minitool, minipump, water bottle, lock, extra tape, and zip-ties (for return shipping). Seal the parts box, and put it in the bottom of the big box, behind where the rear derailleur will be positioned in the box.

6. Remove the front brake, if needed. Take off the front brake and the handlebar or the stem/bar combination if your stem doesn't have a removable faceplate. Remove the front wheel, then hook the bar around the fork.

7. Secure the fork. Slip an old hub or a plastic brace you can get from a bike shop between the drops of the fork to prevent bending.

8. Add padding. Wrap the tubes, fork, and crankarms with pipe foam, bubble wrap, or layers of newspaper.

9. Zip-tie moving parts. Turn the fork around. If you left the stem on, zip-tie it to the top tube. Zip-tie the right crankarm to the chainstay.

10. Slide everything into the box. Nestle the front wheel alongside the main triangle of the frame. Pad every place that metal touches metal. Shake the box and turn it on its side: If you hear metal on metal, pad some more.

11. Add contact info. Write your name and address on each side of the box. Slip your name into the top tube as well. Tape the box shut and reinforce each corner with tape.

filter. Look for a filter with a charcoal core. You can buy a good one for about $75.

More batteries.

Additional maps and reading material. You will appreciate both more than you know.

Photo ID. In addition to your passport, take a second photo ID, such as a driver's license. Keep it somewhere different from your passport.

Toilet paper.

HOW TO PACK

Once you've figured out what to take, you'll need to stow it away. Proper storage will ensure that your bike will steer and stop predictably and will prevent equipment from jostling around—or worse, falling off.

One of the most common setups is a large, heavy rear pannier and a handlebar bag, with no front panniers. However, putting even as much as 10 pounds of weight in a handlebar bag will make your bike less stable and cause it to shimmy on descents. You'll also have very imprecise steering for cornering.

A better way is two sets of medium-to-large panniers (one pair on the front and another on the back), mounted high over the wheels, along with a small handlebar bag. (Where panniers are mounted depends on the type of rack that's attached to your frame. A shorter rack allows panniers to be strapped lower; a longer rack, higher.) This provides more stability and plenty of packing room.

Another system is a small handlebar bag and medium-to-large panniers mounted low on the front and rear. However, this may interfere with heel clearance in the rear if your chainstays aren't long enough. To provide clearance, the bags will likely have to be placed behind the rear axle, which may cause a wagging-tail, whipping action. If you'll be using this mounting system, test-pedal with panniers before a tour.

A final method is to mount medium-size panniers on the front and rear with the rear high and the front low, along with a small handlebar bag. This provides the best combination of handling and packing space.

After you select your rack and pannier system but before you stow anything, think rain. While some panniers tout their waterproof qualities, you should nevertheless take extra measures to ensure that everything you're packing will be safe from the occasional thunderstorm. Line the panniers with trash bags or plastic. Then, buy a large box of zippered plastic bags and slip in everything you're about to put into the panniers. Even if you get soaked to the bone, you'll thank yourself when your banana bread stays dry.

Place larger, heavier items in the lower sections of each bag. Camp stoves and water purifiers fall into this category. While weight is the primary consideration about where to pack equipment in panniers, you should also consider how often or how quickly you'll need to use things. For example, you should put rain gear at the top of the panniers. Your noncycling clothes should also be at the top of the pack so you can slip out of your bike shorts quickly after a day of riding.

A key pannier packing strategy: Arrange items to keep the pannier streamlined—no bulging allowed. Finally, think about balance, not only from side to side but from front to back. You can test the side-to-side balance by holding your loaded bike, letting go, and seeing if it tips to one side or the other. Swap equipment back and forth until the side-to-side balance is close. Also, pick up the front of the bike and then the rear. There should be less weight in the front than in the rear.

CHAPTER 4

Choosing a Bike

and Equipment

How to select a bike and touring accessories for any trip

Here's a little secret about bike touring: You don't have to buy a single thing. If you take nothing else from this book, take this: You absolutely, positively don't need extraordinary equipment to enjoy a bike tour—especially a suppported tour. You don't even need a bike. In fact, you'll save yourself a lot of headaches and often get a chance to ride a high-end bike if you use one provided by a tour company or rent one from a bike shop. Another plus to taking this route is that touring companies and bike shops often know the best setup and kind of bike for the terrain you'll be riding. You just throw a leg over and go, and at the end of the tour, you don't even worry about maintenance.

One small caveat: If you don't already have a pair of padded cycling shorts, invest in some. Yeah, yeah, yeah. You *can* ride without them. But normal shorts or pants have seams that work their way into tender places. That can ruin a tour and keep you off the bike. While a new rider may feel funny about donning tight-fitting bike shorts, they'll save you lots of unnecessary pain. So a beginner who doesn't already have basic cycling equipment should invest in at least one pair of shorts and the other essentials listed in "Everything but the Bike" on page 52.

While you don't *need* any other specialized equipment, there are some touring-specific upgrades that'll make it easier to carry loads or make your trusted old bike more durable. And if you want to take the next step, there are also bikes specifically designed for touring. What makes these bikes worth the bucks is that they're light (a big plus, especially on long climbs or if you have to carry your bike), they're durable (which saves on downtime, spare tires, and aggravation), and they have better styling (hey, why not look good?).

This chapter will explain what makes touring bikes different and better suited for long-haul adventures. We'll walk you through buying the right bike at the right shop and how to fit it to make it comfortable for hours in the saddle. Plus, we'll show you some smart upgrades and what kind of clothing will keep you prepared no matter where you ride.

LONG-HAUL DIFFERENCES

Walk into a bike shop or cruise the Internet, and you'll find many, many touring bike choices. Because there are many forms of touring—from day rides with little need to carry gear to multiday international rides requiring you to be self-sufficient on the other side of the world—there are bikes built to suit each of those specific demands. You should be careful to buy a bike that'll fit your touring needs down the line. For example, on a later trip you might want to expand the amount you'll carry to more than simply a front-of-the-handlebar bag. As with any other bike, you figure out where you can make compromises and what falls into your price range.

Before you plunk down any money, though, you should also know that you don't need a touring-specific bike. The bike that's already in your garage can be used on a tour. Some people ride tours on racing-style road bikes, and mountain bikes can even be a good selection for tours in far-flung places where the roads aren't that smooth.

However, there are advantages to riding a touring-specific bike, such as long-ride-friendly gears and frame geometry that's designed to put you in a more comfortable position than that of other bikes. Here are the things you should look for if you're in the market for a touring bike.

Beefy frame. Tubing should be steel and beefy to prevent wet-noodle handling in corners and to stand up to the additional loads and torque you'll put on the bike. Avoid conventional-diameter aluminum and carbon fiber, though frames built with oversize aluminum and carbon fiber tubes can still work well.

Longer chainstays. This feature allows for a more stable, less bumpy ride because the bike absorbs more of the impact of the road. On a touring bike, the chainstays—the horizontal frame tubes that run from the seat tube to the rear dropouts—will be 17½ to 18 inches long, making the wheelbase 40 to 42 inches. This usually allows you to slip your whole hand between the rear tire and the seat tube. In contrast, on a racing bike, you can barely put a finger in there. A touring bike's longer stays provide more heel clearance so when your foot swings back on a pedal stroke, you won't hit the rear saddlebags. The longer stays also lessen the chain angles produced by a triple crankset; this means less wear and tear on your drivetrain and less chance of chain-suck (the chain getting stuck against the frame). The trade-off for the stability and smoother ride is a larger turning radius. The longer wheel-base also places the weight in any rear panniers ahead of the rear axle. This improves handling, because weight behind the axle would feel like the bike had big, heavy tail wags in corners.

Upright position. Unlike racing-style bikes, which position you in a hunch for more aerodynamics, touring bikes allow a more upright position, more like sitting in a chair. This means you'll have less back strain on long trips. The two main ways a touring bike provides this position is through the head tube angle and a higher stem. A slacker, or lower, angle enables the bike to absorb shock better and positions you more upright. On a touring bike, the typical head tube angle is 71 to 72 degrees. Subtract 1 degree from that range for frames smaller than 21 inches and add 1 degree for frames larger than 25 inches. The higher stem moves your hands up, and along with them your shoulders and

(continued on page 50)

Touring Bike Anatomy

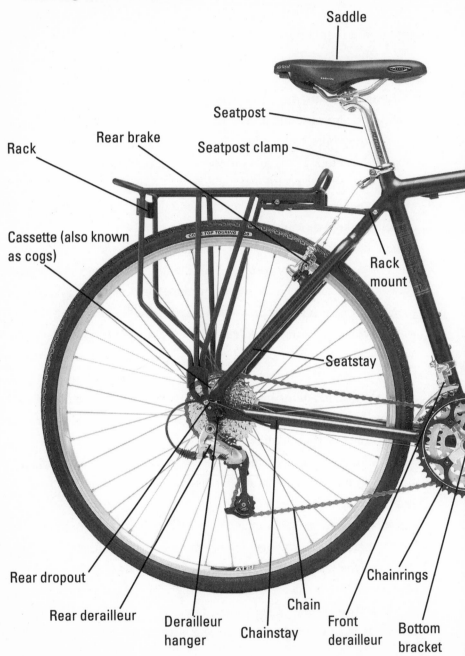

Saddle

Seatpost

Rear brake

Rack

Seatpost clamp

Rack mount

Cassette (also known as cogs)

Seatstay

Rear dropout

Rear derailleur

Derailleur hanger

Chainstay

Chain

Front derailleur

Chainrings

Bottom bracket

Stem

Handlebar

Brake hoods

Brake and shift levers

Headset

Top tube

Cables

Head tube

Front brake

Fork

Front dropout

Down tube

Pedal

Crankarm

Rim

Hub

Spokes

Tire

torso. (See "Fit for You" on page 61 to learn how to fit the bike you select to your specific needs.)

Raked fork. This is the amount of bend, or forward sweep, in the fork. The straighter the fork, the more bumps will be transferred up the bike and to your body. The rake for a loaded touring bike should be 2 to 2¼ inches for a 72-degree head tube angle. Subtract or add ⅛ inch for every greater or smaller degree of head angle. A fork that's raked also helps eliminate toe-wheel overlap, which may make your foot touch the wheel in the 3 o'clock position as you turn. Less bend makes a bike more stable at high speeds and on descents. At lower speeds, such as on most tours, the rake makes the bike more stable, especially with the added weight of any panniers on the front wheel.

Tough wheels. Because it's hard to unweight a loaded bike over bumps, your wheels will take much more abuse. The strongest option is a mountain bike's 26-inch-diameter wheels with slick tires, but that may not fit your bike or needs. For a road touring bike, look for 700C wheels with at least 36 14-gauge spokes and wide, 28c or 32c tires with a puncture-resistant belt under the tread.

Wider tires. The tires on the ideal touring bike are suitable for unpaved roads but not as slow on pavement as the fat tires found on a mountain bike. This is important because most touring is done on paved roads, whether secluded country lanes or designated bike trails. The tires of a mountain bike measure about 50 millimeters wide, while tire width on a touring bike is optimal at 35 millimeters. Racing and sport cyclists might venture as narrow as 20 millimeters but usually stick with about 25 millimeters. You will want a smoother tread than the knobby texture of mountain bikes, with a wide enough tire for traction and puncture resistance. Narrower tires are faster on pavement but perform as well on gravel and damp roads. The wider tires of a touring bike provide more cushioning and comfort on your ride. Inflating your tires to just below the minimum recommended pressure will absorb some of the shock of rougher roads and may reduce the chance of flats.

Hill-busting gears. Look for a bike with three chainrings. The smallest chainring, sometimes called the granny gear, is a welcome addition for hills because it lets you spin in an easy gear while ascending. Touring riders also use lower gears when they are less fresh—say, on the fifth day of a weeklong trip. You'll still have the big rings for the straightaway and downhill speed you may need on the open road. The granny gear should have about 24 teeth. Any size high gear is fine, because descents are good for resting after a climb. And the largest cog on the rear should be about a 28.

Comfortable saddle. A good saddle can mean the difference between a successful tour and a death march. Unfortunately, there's no such device as a butt-o-meter to measure your tush and come up with a precise fit. It's trial and error. Gel saddles can feel good initially, but most riders find that firmer, foam-padded models are better. The gel eventually will conform to your curves down there and end up pressing uncomfortably against you. Some choices you can easily make, such as whether you like more or less padding and a larger or smaller surface area. Women may prefer a wider seat because their sit bones are more widely spaced. Find one you like and put at least 50 miles on it before a tour. Never start a tour with a seat you aren't familiar with. When selecting a rental bike provided by a tour company or cyclery, look for a saddle made by the same company as your own saddle. Even if you can't find the exact model, there will often be ones with similar angles and padding. A bike store might swap a saddle they have on the sales floor, if you ask. Finally, you can pack along your own saddle and ask the rental company or tour operator to install it for you.

Hand-friendly handlebar. Like so many other things on a bike, the kind of handlebar you want depends on what kind of trade-offs you're willing to live with. For example, a flat handlebar will help keep your posture more upright and comfortable in your upper body. But it won't offer many positions and it may quickly make your hands more sore. A drop bar will give you an aerodynamic advantage, saving you time

(continued on page 54)

EVERYTHING BUT THE BIKE

Once you've picked your ride, this handy chart will help you buy the right equipment to go with it.

Accessory	Fit	Function	Form
Helmet	Level on your head, not tilted back or to the side. Ear straps should form an identical V on each side. Should be snug enough that you can slip only two fingers under the chin strap.	Look for the Consumer Product Safety Commission (CPSC) approval sticker to ensure it's safe. Replace if any cracks appear. To keep your head cool, go for one with plenty of vents.	Styles change every year. Whatever you do, don't wear an old-style one that makes you look like a light bulb on two wheels.
Sunglasses	Should not slide off when you shake your head back and forth and up and down. Temples should be snug but not pinching.	UV protection is standard for most lenses. Antifog designs keep you seeing clear even when you're pouring sweat.	Make a statement and adjust to light conditions with a pair with lots of lenses to swap in and out.
Gloves	Should be so snug that the pads can't move around while you're gripping the bar.	Padding keeps your hands—and therefore your whole upper body—fresh.	If you think you can pull off old school, go for the knit, mesh-back models. Otherwise, stick to basic black. Don't try to match 'em with jerseys.

Accessory	Fit	Function	Form
Jersey	Figure out which zipper style you like: half, full, or neckline. The different kinds allow more or less air in, if needed.	Wicking material removes sweat from your body and helps cool you off. Pockets allow handy storage for food or tools.	Avoid: jerseys that are yellow (unless you've led the Tour de France) or feature screaming animals or "witty" slogans.
Shorts	Snug all around your tender parts, with the chamois staying in one place and not shifting while you pedal.	Padded chamois soothes your butt, so instead of going for a gel saddle, opt for a bigger chamois.	Panty or underwear lines are bad. Real bad.
Socks	Length choices include low-rise, ankle, and Pippi Longstocking.	Cycling socks with wicking material remove sweat, keeping your feet cool.	If you are touring internationally and you want everyone to know you're American, wear white socks.
Shoes	Your toes should comfortably fit within the toe box, with room to expand.	Recessed cleats let you walk off the bike without looking like a roller skater on ice.	Turn down the bright colors.
Rain jacket	The rear panel should extend down to cover most of your butt so rain will wash off.	Zippered slots for ventilation allow you to control your inner climate.	Don't go for a yellow-striped jacket unless you have a part-time job on a highway crew.

and energy along the trip, especially on a full day of riding. Also, by allowing you to support some of your weight on your arms, it can help reduce saddle sores.

Performance pedals. As your second most intimate connection to the bike, the pedals are where you put your effort to move and also how you can control the bike on turns. Clipless pedals allow a cleat to click into a mechanism on the pedal body, literally connecting you to the bike. In addition to being able to power the bike through pushing down, these kinds of pedals allow you to pull up. This almost doubles your power and makes you a more efficient rider—very important over a long haul, because you're not fatiguing the same muscles as much. Then, with one flick of the heel, you can disengage the pedal and click out. To learn how to get used to these kinds of pedals, set up your bike in a door frame as you support yourself, then click in and out while the pedals are at different positions. Other pedal options if you need to work up to clipless: toe clips and straps, and flat pedals. The clips and straps provide some benefit from pulling up, but not as much as clipless. Flat pedals are best only for light, easy cruising, because they don't allow you to pull up as part of your pedal stroke and they can allow your feet to slip on any kind of hard effort.

Fenders and mud flaps. If you have ridden in the rain without fenders, you don't need to ask why one might add their extra weight. Your wet back and butt, leading to a chilled body, provide the whole answer. Mud flaps will also help cut down on nasty road spew.

Rack eyelets. These holes on a bike's frame provide the option of carrying the gear you will need for short or long hauls. A rear rack serves as the base for sidebags or panniers, and you can even pile up camping gear on it. If you plan to carry substantial gear, consider a front rack to improve both load balance and handling. Some bikes have seatstay braze-ons that allow a more stable four-point mounting system rather than a three-point arrangement. During installation, secure the rack mounting bolts with thread adhesive, such as Loctite.

Mirror. This is largely a question of personal preference. Does the convenience of glancing back in a mirror outweigh the awkwardness of having one mounted on your helmet or handlebar? Your call. If you don't have enough cycling experience to be comfortable with the alternative—looking back over your shoulder—a mirror is your best option.

Lighting system. A bike light should be included if you'll be riding where it gets dark early. Make sure it takes AA or other easy-to-replace batteries.

BUY BY THE RULES

Now that you know the unique features of a touring bike, you still have to decide which specific bike is right for you. Follow these four rules to help you choose.

Rule No. 1: Know your needs. The last thing you want to think about on a bike tour is your bike. That's not the time to worry about seat angle or wheel grip, or whether a straight handlebar provides enough release points for your aching wrists and arms (the most underrated of all cycling pains). Fret about those things *before* you buy. Ask friends for input, and shop around. Surf cycling sites and send away for catalogs. Figure out how much you plan to carry on the bike. If your touring desires bend only to sag-supported tours (in which a truck or van carries your gear), you have more options at the store. You can consider a sport-tour bike (upright or straight handlebar) or any other type, provided you can enjoy riding it for hours at a time. If you plan to take significant gear on the bike, look more toward the classic touring bike with front and back racks plus slightly wider tires to help bear the load.

Rule No. 2: Take a history lesson. Before making any decisions, review your riding history. If you haven't logged many miles on two wheels, your best bet is to start off on a bike with a flat handlebar and medium-to-wide tires—something closer to a mountain bike than a racing-style road bike. Make sure it has the capacity to upgrade. You can then decide whether you can tolerate the limited number of arm positions available with the flat bar. Chances are the more you tour, the more you will come around to a drop handlebar. While the choice of middleweight tires is likely to be the right one in most cases, you can upgrade those later, too, if the tire width seems to be slowing you down.

Don't fall into the trap of selecting a bike for the type of riding you dream about doing. If you will be averaging two or three times per week on bike paths or easy roads, lighter-wear components (translation: less expensive) will serve your purpose. There is a balance between cheaping out and overspending.

Rule No. 3: Match price to use. You want to find the price point that allows you to get optimal use of your bike. It's a waste to spend a lot of money on a bike and then not ride it regularly. Conversely, saving a couple of hundred dollars on cheaper components will seem like it wasn't such a good idea when you're busted down doing roadside repairs. There are reliable bikes at most any price point, although trade-offs are part of the transaction. "Budgeting for a Bike" on page 58 outlines the kinds of touring bikes and components you can expect to buy at various price points. Remember, you'll spend an additional $200 to $400 for quality accessories, including the minimum of helmet, pump, tool kit, and water bottle and cage, along with shoes and padded shorts.

Rule No. 4: Find a good bike shop. Not all shops cater to, or even know much about, touring cycling. A good way to test whether the shop has touring chops: Ask to see their selection of touring

NOTE ON EQUIPMENT

Equipment changes from year to year. Instead of listing specific bikes or components that may not be available in a year or two, this book will share the desirable and undesirable characteristics. Then, you can do your own comparison shopping.

bikes. If they herd you to mountain bikes or scratch their heads and other body parts, go to another shop. And once you find a shop worthy of your business, follow this checklist for finally purchasing your new bike.

• Value reputation over price. Some new stores undercut the established shops on price, but frequently these startups won't be open in 2 years, because their profit margins will have been too low. You'll have nowhere to go for service or help with warranty issues. On the other hand, established stores offer continuity and some impressive collective years of mechanic experience. Ask other riders where they shop—and why. Listen for raves about good service, knowledgeable staff, and a magic box of parts you can't seem to find elsewhere.

• Deal with knowledgeable salespeople. Your goal is to find the right touring bike for you. It's possible you could draw the one employee in the store who knows racing and not much else. Simply ask for further assistance. The right shop will provide the person who can best help a touring cyclist. Rule of thumb: If you seem to know more than the salesclerk does, that's a bad sign.

• Ask questions. Store personnel can tell if you know your stuff or not. If you don't know something, the good shops will provide the answers with ease and pleasure. Say you'd like to know whether you could get a higher-end frame for better shock absorption without all the higher-end components—you won't find out without asking. If you get jargon for answers, keep questioning until you get the explanation in plain English. If that fails, find another shop.

• Investigate the store's repair shop. Most shops offer a free 30-day tune-up and service discounts for up to a year. You might get free pickup and delivery of your fallen bike. But none of these service goodies mean much if the repair crew is better suited for a *Monty*

BUDGETING FOR A BIKE

Price	Features	Advantages	Disadvantages
Less than $500	Heavy-duty steel or aluminum frame, few suspension options, generic parts that are heavier than desirable for touring, few clipless pedals options	Less money yet plenty of bike for your twice-monthly rides in the neighborhood	Not durable enough to hold up if you ride more frequently
$500– $1,000	Aluminum frame, first level of upper-end components and clipless pedals	Upgraded parts and a bike that should last several years on the road, lighter frame with better chance of full-suspension forks (which hold the wheels in place) for a smoother ride	A bit on the heavy side compared to higher-priced models; might require upgrades if you become enamored with longer rides

Python skit. What to look for: a repair area that appears to be busy but clean. You are likely to smell a faint-to-moderate odor of grease. All good. When to walk: Briskly move toward the exit if the repair crew is one teenager struggling to turn a bike upside down. Untidy surroundings are another bad sign. Good mechanics keep tools in the same places and organize clutter in some fashion.

Price	Features	Advantages	Disadvantages
$1,000– $1,500	Components are mid to high range, featuring better handling and less weight	Upgrade-worthy, high-end aluminum frame that's only appreciated after frequent riding; lighter yet better-performing handlebar and drivetrain	Might still be too heavy for the cyclist who wants to log lots of miles lots of days in a row
$1,500– $2,000	Includes some models with titanium frames, more the rage with racing buffs than touring aficionados	One more step up on components; very light for a touring bike	Hard to say, except maybe you paid for more bike than you really need
$2,000+	Resist bragging to your friends and simply enjoy the smooth ride	Extremely light; knowing you have the best components and features on a bike you'll probably ride the rest of your life	A considerably emptier wallet

• Don't haggle. The markup on bikes isn't very high, so most dealers can't cut much margin. If you mention a competitor's deal (especially if it's a phantom bargain), you may be told to go take that one. Shop owners know what bikes are selling for in their market, and they also know that other shops don't—and can't—discount bikes by hundreds of dollars.

• Look for bargains in the fall and spring. Bike shop workers confide that the best deals are closeouts in the fall months. You can get 10 to 30 percent off overstock bikes and even steeper discounts on summer clothing. In the spring, look to save on winter garb.

• Cut deals on accessories. Most bike shops will bend $10 or $20 here or there on accessories because they are the highest-margin items. But don't expect too much more. Many shops offer discounts on accessories (5 to 10 percent is standard) when you buy a bike, and some owners throw in a helmet to seal the deal.

• Don't go for the quick score. Convincing the owner to throw in a free water bottle cage may offer great instant gratification, but playing it cool can win points with your newfound bike shop pal, who later might just cut your service bill by a significant amount. The right bike shops like to keep regular customers happy; word-of-mouth referrals, not price points, are the lifeblood of the business.

• Know your size or ask to be fitted. The proper fit can take an hour or more. Don't expect the bike shop worker to spend that much time based on the speculation you might buy a bike, but a good shop will take enough time to determine your proper frame size, seat angle, and more. If you don't know your size, don't act like you do. Pretending makes you likely to miss out on some of the best bike and equipment advice you could ever hope to receive.

• Stick to your budget. Store managers report that they perform best when customers are clear about money. Tell them exactly what you're prepared to spend, and you'll be matched up to the best bike for your budget.

• Don't make up your mind before you ride. Test-ride as many bikes as possible, even if only around the parking lot. Some shops may even let you take a bike on a longer test ride. Don't buy a bike you have never tried for at least the proper fit to both your body and your riding needs.

FIT FOR YOU

Finding a comfortable yet effective position on your bike is the most important step in preparing for a bike tour, because the wrong position saps your physical and mental energy. The best way to be properly fitted for a touring bike is to make the right decision at the right bike shop, then ask for an appointment time to fit your new bike. An experienced bike fitter might spend an hour or more with you, tweaking and making the most minute adjustments to specifically tailor your bike to you. Some shops also offer flexibility tests to determine your body's natural position on a bike. Such tests give experienced riders guidance on when resizing is necessary because of lost flexibility from an accident or injury—or gained flexibility from yoga class.

A good tour company will bend over backward to ensure that you have a good-fitting, comfortable bike. They know that if you're uncomfortable on the tour, you'll have a lousy time and be unlikely to take another tour with them, no matter how good the route, sightseeing, and accommodations.

Here's what you should look for when sizing a bike.

Handlebar reach and height. Begin your sizing at a point where you don't feel stretched or bunched up. The bar shouldn't be so low on road bikes that you can't comfortably ride on the drops. A good rule of thumb for bar reach and height is that your arms should form about a 90-degree angle to your torso when your hands are on the hoods. For long-distance touring, you may want to be slightly more upright. Elbows should be slightly bent. If not, your reach is too long or too low. If you're most comfortable resting your hands on the far tips of the brake hoods, your reach is too short. This adjustment can be made by changing the height or length of the stem.

Handlebar angle. Your wrists should be at a comfortable angle when your hands are on the drops or grips. If your wrists are bent, you're going to develop wrist pain. You can change this angle by rotating the angle of the bar back and forth. On a touring bike, the proper position is when the flat part on the bottom of the handlebars is level or pointed slightly down toward the rear end.

Seat height. Just before the pedal reaches the bottom of the downstroke, your leg should be nearly straight—not locked or stretched. If your hips rock up as you pedal, your seat is too high. If you find that your heel automatically drops as you pedal on the bottom of your stroke, your seat is too low.

Fore/aft seat position. Hop on the bike with the crankarms level, keeping your feet in your natural pedaling position in that part of your stroke. Drop a plum line from the front of the bony bump just below your kneecap. The line should bisect the pedal axle or fall within 5 millimeters of the axle. If it's off, loosen the seat clamp and slide the saddle back or forward. Touring cyclists often benefit from being slightly forward to get the glutes (butt muscles) and hamstrings (backs of the thighs) more involved in the pedal stroke. This will make you less tired and achy. And because you'll repeat your stroke maybe thousands and thousands of times, minor changes such as this will pay off on long rides.

Seat tilt. Start with a level saddle. Then experiment with the tilt from there. A downward tilt will relieve pressure on the front of your anatomy. A slight upward tilt will relieve the pressure on your sit bones.

CHAPTER 5

Essential

Touring Skills

Ride safely and with confidence—anywhere in the world

Whoever coined the phrase "It's like riding a bike" probably never cycled up a 5-mile alpine road and then flew back down a dozen hairpin switchbacks. Still, there is truth in that adage: Once you learn how to balance and pedal and brake, you can always return to your two-wheeled friend for another ride no matter how many years you've been away from the saddle. But honing cycling skills—especially for touring cyclists—is underestimated.

When you pick up a few simple tricks, you can save energy while climbing, which gives you stamina to dance the night away or explore a small town instead of collapsing in a hotel room. Learning how to corner and ride in a pack can save you aches and pains, make your riding safer, and make you more confident. Other skills help you in unusual situations, such as when you need to make a panic stop. In becoming a more skilled cyclist, you'll also spare your bike a beating because you'll be able to smooth out rough roads and avoid potholes.

While skills are often underrated, the danger of riding in traffic is often overestimated. By following a few rules and getting clued in on some traffic tricks, you can ride more confidently even in bumper-to-bumper jams. Conquering traffic comes down to being visible, behaving predictably, and believing that you belong in the traffic flow and acting accordingly, instead of thinking of yourself as a nonmotorized inter-loper. When drivers more readily realize you're a part of regular traffic, they're less apprehensive. That makes the roads safer for everyone.

Read on, and ride better and safer.

RIDING SKILLS

While you may have to put in a little saddle time to polish some of your abilities, many of the techniques described in this chapter are ones you'll pick up the next time you ride. Even advanced riders may nab some tips on improving basic skills such as shifting and braking. The following categories are arranged from the most fundamental skills to others that are more specific and used only in certain situations.

Shifting

Some bicycle manufacturers offer newfangled bikes with "automatic shifting" that "shifts for you." Their ads make the whole process of changing gears sound like rocket science. It's not. Clicking a bike into the best gear is pretty easy. First thing, though, before you throw your leg over a bike you're unfamiliar with, check out the shifting levers and brakes. Most road bikes with curled, drop handlebars have shift levers incorporated into the brake levers: Push the lever in and the bike shifts; flick another lever near the brake lever, and you shift back. Some bikes, such as mountain bikes and hybrids, shift using levers you move with your thumb and forefinger. Others are like a motorcycle and have a mechanism on the bar that twists to change gears. If you don't know how the bike you're about to ride shifts, immediately ask the tour guide or someone in the bike shop. As psyched as you may be to start a ride, if you don't know how to shift an unfamiliar bike, you could end up pedaling harder than you need to and become distracted from what's in front of you while you play with gears.

Early in the ride, run the bike through all of its gears so you'll have a sense of their range of ease and difficulty. Remember, the lower-numbered, easy-to-pedal gears are for hills, and the higher-numbered, harder gears are better for flat sections.

Old-school gear-shifting advice was to find a comfortable gear and stay in it. This was because older road bikes had the shift levers mounted on the down tube, which meant you had to take your hand off the handlebar to shift. Since today's bikes put the shift levers at your fingertips, you should shift often to continually adjust the gears to the terrain.

To find out if the gear you're pedaling in is too fast or too slow, you'll need to get a feel for your cadence—that is, your number of pedal revolutions per minute. A good cadence for touring and casual riding is 70 to 85 rpm. (Lance Armstrong, though, regularly tops 120 rpm for extended periods, even up tough Tour de France climbs.) There are cycling computers that measure cadence, but to get a feel for whether you're in the ideal zone, you can just keep an eye on the second hand of your watch and do a little counting. On a flat road with no upcoming turns or hills and little traffic, pedal for 30 seconds, counting the number of complete pedal strokes you make with one of your legs. Double that number and you have your revolutions per minute. In that cadence sweet spot, you'll be spinning 35 to 42 rpm in 30 seconds. If you're slower than that, drop it down a gear or two to spin faster. If you're faster, back off, Lance, and take it easier or click into a slightly harder gear.

THREE SIMPLE SHIFTING RULES

1. Shift into an easier gear before a hill.

2. Low, easy gears are the low numbers; higher means harder.

3. If it's hard to pedal, you're in the wrong gear.

Braking

Just as you make yourself familiar with new shift levers, you should also get the feel of new brakes before riding. Some brakes grab more than others; some are more mushy, requiring more force than other brakes you've ridden. A good initial check to test an unfamiliar bike: Apply the brakes 10 times, and if the levers move back so far that they touch the bar, the brakes are too loose—and potentially dangerous. An easy remedy is to dial out the barrel adjusters where the brake cables enter the levers. That will tighten the cables, giving you more braking power.

Once riding, apply brakes in an on/off, on/off method to avoid over-heating the rims and glazing the brake pads. This kind of feathering (similar to what antilock brakes on a car do) stops you more efficiently and keeps you more in control than just slamming on the brakes does. The increased mass of loaded touring means it takes more time and ef-fort to accelerate and stop, so avoid situations where sudden speed changes are necessary. Also, avoid continually dragging the brakes while riding. Ignoring this advice causes unneeded resistance and wears the brake pads, decreasing their stopping power.

One common mistake when braking is not using the front brake be-cause you're afraid of locking up the front wheel and flipping over the bar. While rolling, your front wheel bears 40 to 50 percent of the weight of you and your bike, but this increases to about 80 percent as deceleration pushes that weight forward. That means the front wheel

---

THREE SIMPLE BRAKING RULES

1. Don't brake while turning.

2. Rear brake first, then front.

3. Feather brakes to avoid locking wheels.

---

also has 80 percent of your braking power. To take advantage of the front brake's power without flipping over the bar, move your weight to the rear and apply the rear brake first, before employing the front.

Before you start emergency braking, set yourself up in a straight line. If you're turning while you try to brake this hard, you'll flip sideways or wash out and skid along the pavement. Your next move is to grab your back brake hard, followed immediately by the front brake. Mash the front brake, but with some modulation, easing the pressure on the back as you increase it on the front. Just don't slam on the front brake first—that *will* send you flying over the bar. Slide to the back of the saddle. The harder you brake, the farther back and faster you should move. Keep control of the bike by extending your arms without locking your elbows. When you're applying both brakes this hard and the rear wheel skids, that means the bike is about to flip. Slightly ease the front brake to regain rear traction. This seems counterintuitive, but it reduces your forward weight while maintaining rear braking power.

Stopping and Starting

About three bike lengths before you have to stop, coast with your right pedal down and free your left foot from its pedal. Unclip if you have clipless pedals, or wiggle out of straps if you ride those. Using the braking technique described earlier, come to a stop, putting your left foot on the ground and lifting yourself off the saddle. By using your left foot, you'll more likely avoid getting a chainring tattoo (brushing your right leg up against the greasy, often dirty chainring). If your bike is loaded, keep it as upright as possible and avoid leaning.

When it's time to get rolling again, spin the pedal so that your dominant, strongest leg will begin the downstroke. This will enable you to more easily start from a stop. If you have to begin from a standstill that's uphill, especially on a steep slope, point the bike so you're headed up the road at a 45-degree angle. You'll have to check for traffic before beginning, but this will enable you to get going.

Cornering

The secret to cornering starts before you're in the turn. Enter a turn at the speed you feel comfortable going through the whole turn. You should be at this speed about three or four bike lengths before the turn begins. If you have to, apply the brakes hard so you don't rocket into a turn. While in the turn, you want to stay off the brakes to avoid skidding out and falling. In addition to adjusting your speed before you enter a turn, you want to take the best line, which is to the outside of the turn, cutting to the apex or center line, then back wide. This reduces the amount of steering and potential jitters and enables you to keep more speed. But because of traffic, you might not be able to take this line.

When cornering on a loaded touring bike, you'll really feel the increased weight (as much as 75 pounds for bike and baggage). Chapter 7 includes some training tips that will help you build the strength you'll need to optimize handling, but you should also master the following cornering techniques.

Control the bike by leaning and using your body to swoop the bike through the turn. A loaded bike is more prone to sliding out in a turn, so go slower and lean less than you normally would. And don't jack your handlebar around—doing so often leads to having to swerve back to overcompensate, making you look like a DUI driver to the cars behind you. This is a case where the old-school way is still the best way: Point your inside knee to the apex of the turn while your outside pedal is down. You're sort of making an outrigger with your body to use weight, rather than turning the bar, to move around the corner.

Here are three other ways to roll through turns, depending on the conditions.

1. Sharp turns and in groups. A turning technique called countersteering enables you to maneuver through tight turns and quickly adjust your line in a crowd of other riders. You begin countersteering about two wheel lengths from the turn by pushing down or pulling back sharply on the handlebar on the opposite side you want to turn. For example, push down on the right side of the bar if you want to turn left. Your bike will slightly veer away from the turn, then dive back the correct way. Look through the corner, focusing on the exit point. Your outside leg should be pressing down and straight. For the best control, start the turn with your hips slightly to the rear of the saddle. While going through the turn, your bike and lower body will lean into the corner while your upper body leans the opposite way. Adjusting this balance allows you to change the line as you move around the corner. As you begin the turn, push your inside knee against the top tube. Adjusting pressure here helps control your line. The more pressure, the sharper the turn. With less pressure, you go wider and more upright.

2. Over oil or gravel. This kind of turn is called steering, where you use more of a turn of the handlebar to negotiate the turn. While this turning method provides added stability on sketchy surfaces, it's harder to change your arc once you start your turn, so don't use this technique if you're near other riders. First, keep your speed at 15 mph or less. Anything faster and you'll risk losing traction on the slippery stuff. Move forward until your nose is aligned with the inside brake lever. While keeping the bike upright, nearly perpendicular to the ground, with only a slight lean in toward where you're turning, lean your body into the turn so much that you straighten your outside arm. Twist your hips into the turn and move the bar by pulling back or up on it with

---

FIRST COMMANDMENT
OF CORNERING

Thou shalt not put the inside pedal down. If you break this commandment, you could catch the corner of the pedal on the ground, and nothing ruins a vacation like road rash.

---

your inside arm, elbow bent, while pushing out or down on the bar with the outside arm. Keep your knees in and continue pedaling.

3. In wet weather. On wet asphalt or in a long turn where you can't see the exit, this turning technique—called inclination—gets you through safely with loads of traction. It keeps your weight planted on the saddle and uses the force of the turn to keep the tires on the road. First, lean into the turn while staying centered over the bike—you and the bicycle will be leaning at the same angle. Straighten your outside knee and press down with significant force, like you're trying to break off the pedal. Press your inside knee against the top tube. This is especially important on a wet surface, when you don't want to use the bar to steer and adjust your line through the curve. Decrease pressure on the inside knee and the bike will right itself. Increase pressure and you tighten the turn. Gently pull up with your outside hand.

Climbing

On a tour, you're usually not worried about speed, and you might be loaded with panniers or other equipment, so you'll likely be tackling all your climbs in the seated position. On seated climbs, you'll get more power and more efficient energy transfer if your weight is slightly forward on the saddle. If you don't have weight on your front wheel, such as panniers or a handlebar bag, grip the bar so your hands are about a thumb's length from the stem on either side. Put the heel of your hand on the bar and wrap your fingers loosely. When there is weight on your front wheel, you want to keep your hands out farther on the bar to help balance.

When climbing while sitting, tension can cause neck pain and headaches. Relax by stretching your fingers, arms, shoulders, and neck at least every 30 minutes. It also helps to stand on your pedals and stretch your legs when you reach a flat spot to get a break from climbing.

On a really steep hill, or if your butt and legs need a break from

THREE WAYS
TO CONQUER ANY CLIMB

1. Pick an object alongside the road and just concentrate on making it to that point; once you make it, pick another goal farther up.

2. Ride at a pace you feel like you can maintain all day.

3. Save your energy for the top; don't ride fast at the base, or else you'll blow out when the going gets steeper.

seated climbing, you may climb while standing. Especially on a loaded bike, keep the bike upright and steady, rather than rocking it from side to side. When standing, keep your head up and chest out and even with or slightly behind the point where the stem clamps the bar. This allows you to breathe easier and also lets you use your body's weight to move the pedals, instead of relying only on muscle. While standing and climbing, don't lock your arms; keep a slight bend in them. Use your butt to power standing climbs by angling your torso so it feels like you're getting up out of a chair, instead of about to sit. You'll get more power and more efficient transfer when your butt muscles aren't bent. As you pedal, pull your leg up and wrap it over the top of the stroke. Imagine you're running and bringing your leg around for the next step. This pulling up gives you balance and power through your stroke.

Descending

Controlling your descending speed begins at the top. If you allow the bike to get rolling fast early on a long descent, the momentum will make it harder to stop and control the bike. So adjust your speed by braking hard and early on a descent, instead of riding your brakes all the way down. On really steep, long hills, riding the brakes too long can overheat the pads, dramatically reducing your braking power and maybe even popping your tire (since the rims and tires also heat up).

Sometimes the bike will begin to wobble as you head downhill. To steady it and increase control, level your pedals and clamp your knees to the top tube. You can also use your knee to steer the bike, since moving the bar can be risky at higher speeds. To move the bike left, add pressure to the top tube with your right knee.

Finally, when descending at the same speed as traffic, go ahead and take up the center of the lane. That'll prevent cars from passing you and going even faster than they should anyway.

Group Riding

The most essential skill when in a pack of other riders is holding a straight line and not swerving in corners or around obstacles. As mentioned in the section on cornering, you can stay steady in turns by clamping your knees to the top tube and using weight, instead of the handlebar, to steer. To steer right, press your left leg against the frame. Press your right leg to turn left.

To avoid swerving around obstacles, practice unweighting the front and then rear wheel on training rides as you roll over impediments.

If you ride in groups often, you're eventually going to bump other riders. First, don't panic. Just because you touch doesn't mean you'll take a spill. While it might sound counterintuitive, you should lean into the other rider. This will stabilize both of you and allow both of you to get over that initial jolt of contact and keep rolling for a while. Then slowly roll apart by leaning away from each other, without swinging your handlebars to turn. If the other rider falls, fight your instinct to immediately stop and check on him or her. Continue riding straight and be sure there's no traffic behind you before you swing around.

Communicating with your fellow riders can help you avoid bumping and other mishaps. Here are five ways to talk with your hands, plus two ways to make what comes out of your mouth much clearer.

Signal a left turn: Point your left arm straight out.

Signal a right turn: Point your right arm straight out. Motorists signal a right turn by sticking out a left arm and bending it down, but that's only because they can't reach across the seat and out the right-hand side window.

Indicate a slowing pace to the riders behind you: Bend one arm down at the elbow and slowly flap your hand backward.

Indicate hazards: Point out obstacles such as potholes by pointing down toward them with whichever hand is closer to them. Begin pointing before you pass the hazard, not as you pass. Don't overuse this signal by pointing out every twig and crack in the road.

Signal pulling off: When you're leading a paceline and ready to pull off, flap your fingers out to the side while your hands remain on the bar.

Give traffic warnings: Saying "car back" or "car up" is much clearer than simply "car."

Indicate passing intentions: Saying "on your left" is best when you're about to pass another rider or a pedestrian. Just saying "left" might make some riders swerve to the left, thinking that's where you're telling them to go.

Drafting

A specific group riding skill is drafting, where you're following a lead rider's rear wheel fairly closely. You can save up to 40 percent of your energy by drafting, plus it's a good skill to have when you have to ride in close quarters. With your hands on the hoods or drops, where you can reach the brakes if necessary, ride 6 to 12 inches behind your leader's wheel. Learning to hang steady can be hard, and while you're learning, you'll yo-yo: first too close, then too far. So other riders won't call you Duncan (like the yo-yo—get it?), try this: When you're about

DRAFTING DO'S AND DON'TS

You should follow these etiquette tips—especially when you don't know the riders you'll be drafting.

Do

- Latch on to a rider who follows a steady line and has a smooth pedal stroke.

- Initiate contact by pulling alongside, nodding, and politely asking to hang out on his rear wheel.

- Moderate your speed by sitting up into the wind or soft-pedaling.

- Take your turn at the front to pull for as long as previous riders have.

- Climb politely by leaving extra space between wheels, because sometimes wheels lurch back when going from sitting to standing.

Don't

- Draft someone who swerves, has a choppy stroke, or does bone-headed stuff like drink in the middle of a pack.

- Sneak onto someone's wheel when they don't know you're there.

- Space out while staring at your leader's wheel.

- Brake, speed up, brake, speed up, brake.

- Stay up front too long, get tired, and slow the pack. If you can't pull for as long as the other riders, shoot for half as long but at the same speed.

6 inches from the wheel, stop accelerating but keep lightly spinning the pedals. Let your momentum take you slightly closer, then ease pressure back into your pedal strokes until your pace matches your lead rider's.

When you're drafting, you need to be alert for what the rider in front is doing. For example, if the rider stands to climb or sprint, the rear wheel of the bike will shoot backward toward you by 3 to 6 inches. To avoid touching wheels, keep a line that's a tire width to either side of the lead wheel. Maintain a pace that'll avoid allowing that wheel to overlap yours. Don't become fixated on the wheel you're following. Instead, look 20 to 30 feet beyond the rider directly in front of you so you spot upcoming hazards, terrain changes, or action in the group of riders.

Swerving

To avoid a hazard, such as a pothole or a car that's cutting you off, ride around by quickly countersteering. The countersteer uses your weight to start the turn. Push your handlebar left to start a right turn. Push on the right bar to start a left-hand turn. By nudging the wheel initially opposite of the direction you'll be turning, you make your bike swoop back the other way, the direction you want to turn.

Unweighting

This easy-to-learn skill can save you many flat tires and possibly other, more serious damage to your bike when you have to roll over rough roads or encounter unexpected potholes. With your pedals level, as you roll up on a pothole, you can ride over it as lightly as possible by pressing down on your front wheel about a wheel length before the pothole, then lifting up your front wheel as it passes over, then unweighting your rear wheel by leaning slightly forward of the saddle. This move reduces the amount of pressure and weight you're placing on each tire, which may save your tubes and help you avoid denting your rims and breaking spokes.

Looking Back

Being able to look behind you without swerving in traffic is an essential skill. While mirrors on your bike or helmet can help you see the coming traffic, being able to turn your head and make eye contact with drivers is important in avoiding accidents and communicating where each of you is going. Practice riding straight on the painted lines of a low-traffic street or in a parking lot. Once you feel comfortable riding in a straight line while continuing to pedal, keep on the line while turning your head to the left. Slightly drop your left shoulder while keeping your right shoulder level. You should be able to turn your head far enough to look to the side and slightly back. Another quick way to learn: On a smooth road with no traffic, point your left arm straight back at a tree or sign that's behind you, then turn your head and neck as you look back, sighting down your arm, which will help you ride straight. Do this for only a second or two at a time. Work up to where you can do it for 3 or 4 seconds. Then, forget the pointing part and just start looking back.

Pacing

One of the biggest (and most common) mistakes of novice touring cyclists is going too fast too early on a trip, or struggling to keep pace with a group that's a lot faster. The best way to avoid wasting your energy too early is to find people riding at your pace and stick with them. Don't constantly try to catch up with faster riders.

In the Rain

The most dangerous time to ride in the rain is the first 10 minutes after it starts. That's when the water picks up oils and spreads them across the road. Oil tends to collect in the middle of the road, so keep to one side even when you're riding in the center of the lane. If you have to ride over a slippery surface, stop pedaling, level your pedals, keep your weight centered over the bottom bracket, stay off the brakes,

TOP 10
BEGINNER TOURING MISTAKES

1. Inadequate training

2. Riding too hard at the beginning of the trip

3. Pushing too-hard gears

4. Not shifting enough

5. Bringing too many dressy clothes

6. Being unprepared for cold

7. Not eating or drinking enough while riding

8. Not tuning the bike before the trip

9. Not being flexible in planning

10. Making the trip a race instead of a relaxing vacation

and flex your elbows and knees as momentum carries you through. When riding through a turn, use the slower but safer turning technique of keeping your bike perpendicular to the ground and leaning your body while taking the long line to the outside of the turn.

When the going gets wet, avoid riding over road lines. Stirred into the ingredients of thermoplastic road-line strips are tiny, spherical glass beads designed to refract headlights. That is good for visibility but makes a very bad riding surface, because the beads reduce friction, making the paint slipperier than the pavement.

Two other things that become lots more dangerous when wet are metal, such as train tracks or road plates, and leaves. When crossing these hazards in the rain, maintain a straight line and avoid braking and turning.

In wet weather, your brakes will take longer to slow you down, so you must anticipate your need to brake. Apply the brakes earlier than normal so they have a chance to squeegee off the rims before you really need your stopping power. A good rule of thumb: Allow twice your normal stopping distance when braking in the rain. To speed up the squeegee process, you can ride the brakes for 10 seconds while pedaling. Pedaling also keeps your bike more stable in the wet stuff and keeps your natural rhythm and momentum going. Also anticipate suddenly grabby brakes. Once the water is sluiced off, the brakes might suddenly get big power. Be ready to loosen your grip. And when riding through wet stuff, relax. You have nearly as much traction on wet roads as you do on dry.

Against a Headwind

Nothing will make you feel slower and stretch a hill out longer than a stiff headwind. To cut through the wind, think of yourself as a bag that you want to close off to prevent wind getting in. Lower yourself over the handlebar with your hands on the drops or hoods, and bend your elbows so they're almost at 90 degrees and flanking your sides. Float your chin over the stem as you look up the road.

In a Crosswind

In a crosswind, you need to stay relaxed, because if you stiffen your arms and back, you'll be more easily moved by the wind. On a bike with a drop handlebar, put your hands on the drops. This will make you more stable and put your hands in the best position to react when the wind changes. As you pedal, lean slightly into the wind, 2 or 3 degrees from vertical. The harder the wind, the more lean you want to have. If you get blown to the side by a gust, steer back by swiveling your hips or leaning into the wind. Resist the temptation to just swing the handlebar to get you back on line—moving the bar will make you weave.

When the wind is from your right, move to the right edge of the road. Moving over puts you closer to fences and trees that act as a barrier from the wind, decreasing how it affects your riding. And when you're to the right, swerving because of a sudden gust of wind won't push you into oncoming traffic.

With wind from the left, ride maybe a foot or more to the left of where you normally would, to prevent rolling off the road when a gust comes along.

Through Snow

To help improve traction in snow, lower the tire pressure 10 to 15 psi below normal. Then, to steer through the white stuff, stay seated and center your weight over the bottom bracket. If you're too far back, the rear wheel will bog down. If you're too far forward, your front wheel may plow into the snow instead of skimming through it.

When turning, instead of making wide swings of the handlebar, use your body to take turns wide. Shift your hips on the saddle so that your thigh on the inside of the turn moves back on the saddle and your thigh on the outside moves forward. This twisting motion will help steer the bike without risking your front wheel washing out. You'll still probably skid a little, though.

When the thermostat is below freezing, beware of ice patches. Sometimes they'll be dark places on the road or trail, similar to the black ice that motorists are warned about in the winter. To get over an ice patch without taking a spill, first let the bike go where it wants to and don't hit the brakes. A jerk will send you and the bike flying. If you spot the ice before you're on it and have time to steer, set up so that you ride straight across it, instead of trying to turn in the middle of the slippery stuff.

Since ice and water may accumulate on your brakes and rims, allow for triple your normal stopping time. This is also a good idea because bulky gloves can't give you the same feel on the brakes.

SAFELY NEGOTIATING TRAFFIC

Riding in traffic can be scary—several thousand pounds of vehicle zoom down roads at speeds up to five times faster than your bike. This fear factor quickly diminishes with a little know-how. Here's how to sail through traffic in a variety of situations.

Just Beginning

To get more used to weaving around cars, go to a grocery store parking lot and negotiate traffic there. You'll get used to the cars and avoid panicking even when you're in bumper-to-bumper jams.

Commiserating with Other Cyclists

When touring with a partner with a different level of cycling expertise, ride in traffic together, taking turns leading and following. From the back, the more experienced rider can figure out what a newbie leading rider can do to be safer. When the more practiced rider is in front, the less-experienced rider can imitate what the veteran does.

Looking Ahead

Always scan 30 to 50 feet ahead of you, looking for hazards, keeping an eye out for traffic, planning for turns, and allowing yourself plenty of time for braking. In heavy traffic, scan two or more cars ahead for exhaust smoke that indicates acceleration or deceleration. Also, a car that's slightly shaking as it goes along the road in front of you may mean potholes are ahead. Remember that vehicles often fail to signal, but by keeping an eye on drivers' heads and which way they look, you can determine which way they're turning.

In addition to looking ahead on the road, keep an eye on the sidewalk for pedestrians. Continuously split your attention among the line ahead, your escape route if blocked, side streets, and the sidewalk. Watch for the unexpected. Perhaps the pedestrian walking on the sidewalk will try to cross against the light in front of you because he doesn't see any cars.

Taking the Right of Way

Take your share of the road. In most situations, ride in the right lane but as far to the left as is practical. You may be slightly more in the flow of traffic, but that's safer, because you're more visible and less likely to run into grates or debris along the side of the road.

On streets with curbs, ride at least 2 feet away from the curb so your pedal doesn't clip it. On wide roads with broad, clean shoulders and no rumble strips, ride just outside the traffic lane.

On narrow or busy roads, ride just inside the traffic lane (about 6 inches to the left of the right-hand lane line) so cars must go partially over the middle line to pass. This prevents drivers from remaining in the right lane and squeezing by you. When a road is so narrow that an overtaking car must use the left lane, you should ride more in the center of the right lane.

Sometimes a driver will squeeze past you and then cut you off to turn right. The car will probably drift to the center as it approaches the intersection, setting up for a quick turn. Maintain your line and make eye contact with the driver to ensure you don't get cut off.

Don't weave back and forth into and out of parking spaces or the shoulder. Continuing in a straight line will make you more predictable to drivers.

When low visibility is a problem, such as in rain, in fog, or at dusk, don't ride more than 3 feet to the right of traffic. A driver's line of sight is 20 to 30 degrees from straight ahead. Bright jerseys and stylishly placed reflective tape can light you up and make you more noticeable.

Alongside Cars

Make eye contact with drivers. When you look at them, you can signal intentions and determine whether they know you're riding there.

TAKE 'EM ALONG—APPROPRIATELY

Introducing a significant other to an activity that's an important part of your life is always tricky—even more so when it's a physical activity such as cycling. When people are turned off by cycling, it's not usually because they don't like riding—it's because their first experience is too hard. A first ride or tour that goes through heavy traffic, up steep climbs, or through rainy weather will be more torture than fun. Here are a few guidelines to improve your loved one's tour (and the rest of your lives once you get home).

Selecting a Tour

Easy does it. To increase the possibility of more rides and tours, err on the side of cushy tours.

Rest often. Stop frequently to take pictures, rehydrate, and eat.

Selecting Clothing

Encourage dressing in character. If your partner is up for the full-on ensemble, power on. If not, don't push him or her into Lycra.

Nodding your head in the direction you're going, making hand signs, and waving also can make riding safer.

Turning

Crossing paths with a car is a more common source of accidents than being rear-ended. This is most likely to happen at intersections and driveways, where drivers turn across the road. One problem may be that drivers can't estimate your speed, especially if you're coming down a descent. Sit up and keep your hands on the levers, ready to brake.

Use your position in the lane as a signal of where you'll be turning. Use the left part of the lane when you're preparing to merge

Just make sure the clothing isn't binding or so loose that it'll tangle in the bike.

But make the case for cycling shorts. If your honey just doesn't go for it, suggest wearing them under regular shorts. A sore, chafing crotch does not make for a romantic touring vacation.

Check the weather forecast. You might be experienced enough to gut it out in cold rain, or sweat through unexpected heat waves, but your tour will turn ugly awfully quickly if your newbie partner gets too hot or cold.

Looking for Bad-Time Warning Signs

Check for white knuckles. They're a sign that the new rider is too tense, so suggest a lighter grip or lightly drumming fingers on the bar.

Discourage sitting over bumps. Suggest standing on the pedals.

Watch for locked elbows. Show how elbows should flex to act as shock absorbers.

or turn left. The center is for when you are traveling straight and need to take the lane for safety, such as on tight roads or fast descents; ride fast enough that you don't slow traffic. The right side of the road is for turning right or allowing cars to pass. If you can't get into the right lane to make a turn, don't force it by cutting across traffic. Continue straight through the intersection and double back when traffic clears.

Always signal turns. Work into the lane you want to be in at about 150 feet before the upcoming intersection. To signal your turn, hold up your arm so it's level with your shoulder, and point. This is a clear signal and won't confuse drivers. Signal your turn until you get into the intersection, then return both hands to the bar to maintain control as you turn.

Take precautions to avoid getting hit when you turn left. You'll be less likely to get hit by opposing traffic if you follow a car closely, by about 6 feet or so, through the turn. Otherwise, wait for a break in traffic before going. Opposing drivers time their left turns for after the last car. They might not see you. So to make your own left, stick very close to—perhaps even pull up alongside—a car in front of you that's also going left. Or slow and be prepared to brake. Also, stand on the pedals to increase visibility.

Changing Lanes

Change lanes smoothly. Scan behind you, looking over the shoulder that's closest to the lane you want to shift to. If there's traffic closer than six to eight car lengths, signal by pointing. Cross into the new lane and ride on the right third of it.

Crossing in Front of Driveways and through Intersections

Watch for cars edging out of driveways and into intersections. Drivers will test traffic openings by sticking their noses out into traffic, often with limited visibility. When you approach such areas, stand on your pedals and make eye contact. After checking for traffic behind you, move to the center of the lane.

Alongside Parked Cars

Don't get doored. Ride 3 to 4 feet from parked cars. Look for people inside and for brake lights.

Rush-Hour Traffic

Read the cars. Look at front wheels. Are they turning? Look in windows. Has the driver shifted his hands to a different part of the steering wheel? If so, he's going to turn.

Plan escape routes. Sometimes motorists misjudge your speed or just don't see you. Assume cars will turn in front of you, and plan a way around them.

Assert yourself. When you're traveling at the speed of traffic or even faster, take up the lane. But stay on the right if traffic is moving faster than you are. Be aggressive, not risky. Don't blow through traffic lights and stop signs or swerve around slow cars.

Sidewalk Riding

Sometimes you may have to ride on sidewalks. When you do, remember that you're a guest. When passing pedestrians, don't ring or shout when you're within 5 feet of them—you'll just scare them. You should make your presence known from 15 to 20 feet away by ringing your bell or announcing on which side you intend to pass. And don't ride close to them, waiting to pass. That's rude. When walking your bike, be aware of the bar and chainring. You don't want to poke a ped or give him a chainring tattoo.

CHAPTER 6

Off-Road Tours and Essential Mountain Biking Skills

For a way-out-there vacation, take it to the trails

As the mountain biking craze increased in the 1980s, new tour options opened up. With its wider, knobby tires and its suspension, the mountain bike allowed cyclists to reach parts of the world where the closest pavement was hundreds of miles away. On an off-road vacation, you can dip into secluded hot springs, then ride back to luxury hotels at night. Or you can camp out along high-plains trails that are marked only by signposts on the next horizon. Guided group mountain bike tours have evolved, too. Some provide showers and serve gourmet cuisine after a hard day of riding through deep woods.

While on a mountain bike tour, you'll see amazing terrain that those who stick to roads don't get a chance to experience. However, you'll also have to ride through that same terrain. That means having some rudimentary mountain biking skills and doing some additional planning and packing.

No matter what kind of tour you're planning, it's good to know what to expect. On a mountain bike tour, appropriate expectations and preparation may be a matter of survival. You'll be farther away from civilization and emergency assistance. And if you plan your own mountain bike tour, you'll have to be sure you can handle the mileage and carrying all your supplies. Along with explaining what to expect on a mountain bike tour, this chapter also includes smart gear additions for taking it off road and explains some essential mountain bike riding skills. While you may not need to learn how to jump a log on every tour, the skills you can add will make your ride smoother, help you avoid taking spills, and save your energy.

MOUNTAINOUS EXPECTATIONS

Compared to road tours, the average daily mileage for mountain tours is usually less, yet you may still be on the bike for about the same amount of time per day. Riding is slower because the terrain is tougher. You'll likely be riding over either singletrack or fire roads. Singletrack is a narrow trail, usually between 4 and 18 inches wide, on which only one rider at a time can roll along. This thin ribbon of trail, though, is how bicyclists can ride to the most remote areas and intimately experience the countryside. You'll appreciate the contours of the mountains and get to know the vegetation—because you'll be riding over, next to, and through it. Along with roots and logs, other obstacles such as rocks, ruts, and drop-offs are common on singletrack. However, some singletrack trails are smoother and perfect for new riders or first-time mountain bikers.

Fire roads are packed dirt with few large obstacles. They are often service routes for forest vehicles (hence the name) and other motorized all-terrain vehicle traffic. These roads often have steep pitches and sharp U-bends as they snake up the mountains. Because there are no technical obstacles, fire roads can be used to ride uphill before rolling onto the real lure of mountain biking, singletrack, on the way down.

Knowing the length and technical challenges of a tour in advance will enable you to train and prepare beforehand. The best way to learn the difficulty of a trail is to ask at a local bike shop, or if you're hiring a touring company, to check the daily itinerary so you can match your skills to the ride. Some supported tours are strictly for fit riders with advanced mountain biking skills; others can be ridden by people getting on a bike for the first time. Good companies that have done their homework will know how tough the trails are. Some even assign difficulty rankings similar to ski mountains' diamond system. Steer clear of any company that's ambiguous about the difficulty of a mountain bike tour. While many tour companies have support and sag wagons to haul you back, you're often on singletrack that's pretty far from any road. So you need to count on riding yourself in *and* out.

When planning your own mountain tour, your options are similar to those of do-it-yourself road touring. You and a group of friends can rent a condo near one of the prime mountain biking destinations, such as Moab, Utah; Slatyfork, West Virginia; or Mount Snow, Vermont. Use the house as a base and take trails from there, returning at night to the comfort of showers, warm beds, and a Jacuzzi. You can also pack along tents and sleeping bags and plan a route that's a large loop, where you start and end at the same place. Or, with a little planning and shuttling, you can take a route from point A to point B, connecting the dots by riding from hotel to hotel, hut to hut, or campsite to campsite. In case you don't have a friend to help with shuttling bikes and bodies, bike shops often have shuttle services. The truly ambitious can ride the longest mountain bike route in the world—the Great Divide Mountain Bike Route from Canada to Mexico.

OFF-ROAD EQUIPMENT

You'll need some specialized gear for the great outdoors. Obviously, the first necessity is a bike, be it your own or a loaner from the touring company. Here's how a mountain bike differs from a road bike.

Mountain Bike Components

Handlebar. A flat or straight handlebar allows fewer change-of-grip possibilities than a road bike's curved bar. This means padded gloves are even more important. For longer tours, you can add bar ends that provide additional positions and help with climbing.

Suspension fork. Snagging motorcycle technology, a mountain bike has a front fork that moves up and down as the front wheel rolls over obstacles. The latest designs compensate for different types of terrain, absorbing big bounces and smoothing out the ride over even washboard-type trails. Some forks include features such as adjustable travel, meaning you can modify how far the fork moves, to allow for more or less aggressive riding styles; others include lock-outs that keep them from bobbing on climbs.

Rear suspension. Some mountain bikes have a rear shock that also acts to soak up bumps. On most dual-suspension bikes, rear travel can range from 1 to 6 inches, with the lower end of travel for smoother, more cross-country-type trails, and the greater travel for big drops and going faster over washboard-type terrain. In general, the more suspension, the heavier the bike. If you think there's a lot of off-road touring in your future, find a shop that rents bikes with different suspensions and try 'em out. Find one that suits your riding style, comfort level, and regular destinations.

Knobby tires. Most mountain wheels are 26 inches from side to side, as opposed to the larger road standard of 700c. The knobs provide additional grip over slick roots and other trail obstacles. To make a mountain bike more road-friendly, swap the knobbies for slicks.

Baggage

On a guided tour, the tour company will likely shuttle your stuff, so you won't need to worry about additional equipment to transport supplies. But if you plan your own mountain bike trip, figuring out how to carry your stuff is a necessity. Here are your options.

Racks. Because of suspension systems, racks for mountain bikes have to be specially designed. A front rack attaches to the brake mount and the front wheel quick-release. On a hardtail bike (one without rear suspension), you can attach a rack in much the same way that you would on a road bike. For a full-suspension bike, look for a rear rack that attaches to the seatpost alone. While it won't hold as much weight as others, it will provide some additional packing space.

Panniers. It's okay to use panniers if you'll be on a fire road, but on a narrow, technical trail, they'll snag on rocks and tree branches. Saddlebags also make your bike harder to carry over obstacles. Instead, strap some gear to a rear rack and pack the rest in an internal-frame backpack.

Trailer. On a mountain bike, many riders find that having weight on the bike or even in a backpack reduces handling and makes it difficult to ride over even small obstacles. One solution that allows for plenty of packing room is a trailer that attaches to the bike and rolls behind. A mountain bike trailer comes with knobby tires and suspension. You pull the load and it bounces happily and safely behind.

Clothing

Once you've outfitted your bike, you can do the same for yourself. Here's some trail-friendly clothing you might like to have.

Helmet. A road helmet will work for mountain riding. A helmet specifically designed for off-roading may have a visor to keep the sun out of your eyes. Choosing your headgear is more about style than about function. The one thing to remember: Because you might take more spills on a mountain bike, always inspect your helmet after a fall, even just a small one. If there's the slightest crack, replace the helmet.

Shorts. Here's another equipment choice that's largely about personal preference. Mountain biking shorts are baggier than road shorts and have pockets, but they still include the chamois. You may even want to wear baggies for road touring since the pockets and non-skintight ap-

(continued on page 94)

Mountain Bike Anatomy

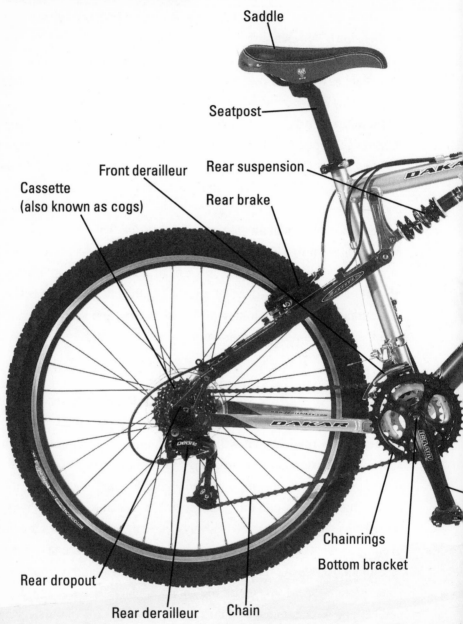

Saddle

Seatpost

Front derailleur

Rear suspension

Cassette
(also known as cogs)

Rear brake

Chainrings

Bottom bracket

Rear dropout

Rear derailleur

Chain

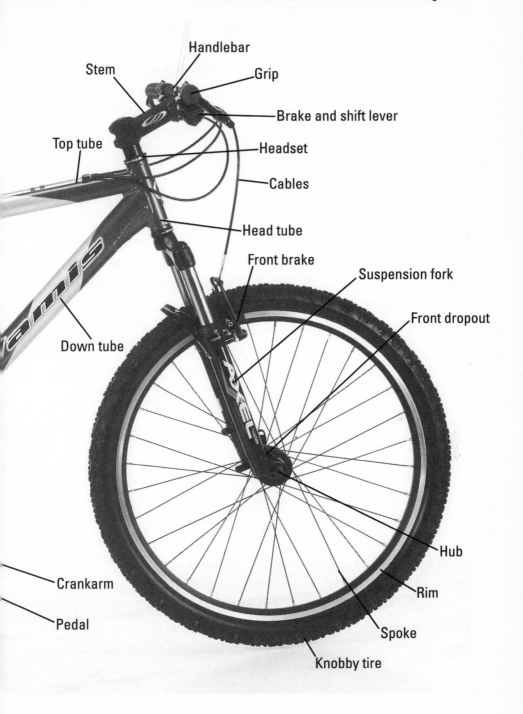

Handlebar

Stem

Grip

Brake and shift lever

Top tube

Headset

Cables

Head tube

Front brake

Suspension fork

Down tube

Front dropout

Crankarm

Hub

Pedal

Rim

Spoke

Knobby tire

pearance lets you walk around off the bike and go into restaurants and other public places without your attire screaming, "Cyclist!"

Gloves. While you can certainly use road gloves off road, mountain bike gloves come with long fingers that help protect your digits on those small spills. The padding may also be cushier to offset the limited number of grip positions on the mountain bike handlebar.

Hydration system. A backpack with a bladder that you can fill with water allows you to sip from a tube without taking your hands off the bar—a big plus when steering around and riding over obstacles on the trail. Also, this means you don't have to deal with water bottles rattling around in and bouncing out of their cages. When you need to pack in as much as possible, though, it's still a good idea to add water bottles.

Shoes. Emphasized treads give mountain biking shoes traction on trails when you need to push the bike or walk sections. Also, look for waterproof features if you'll be riding into wet conditions.

ESSENTIAL MOUNTAIN BIKING SKILLS

For most guided mountain bike tours, you probably don't have to learn new riding techniques, because you can select a tour that's appropriate for your experience level. But to minimize the need to push your bike and to increase the enjoyment of your tour, here are the 10 most important things to learn before you head to the singletrack. A big bonus: You can transfer your newfound skills to the road, where you'll be better able to handle unexpected obstacles, you'll be more balanced through turns, and you'll stop faster without falling.

Float on that thin line. By riding in what many describe as "the attack position," you can more easily change your line, adjust to terrain, and make the ride softer on your tender parts. Your elbows should be bent and out slightly from your sides. When you're not pedaling, the pedals should be level and your knees bent, ready to act as additional

---

BEST MOUNTAIN BIKING ADVICE FOR FIRST-TIMERS

Ride in a group. The more people you're with, the more you'll discover about the terrain. You'll see the riders ahead of you take bad lines and mess up, then you'll be able to avoid their mistakes. In a group, you can also follow someone who's ridden the trail before, or who's at least been mountain biking for a while. Stay 10 to 15 feet behind the rider in front of you, and don't become so fixated on following his wheel that you don't look ahead on the trail. Constantly scan about 30 feet ahead, then glance back down to see the lead rider's line. Mimic the line he rides and pay attention to when he shifts gears and brakes. You'll be saved from unexpected gear shifts, you'll ride smoother lines, and you'll see when it's best to brake.

---

shock absorbers. To float and be light on your bike, don't allow all your weight to be in one area. Split your weight among your feet, hands, and butt. While you may occasionally stand on the pedals, if you spend too much time standing, you'll waste a lot of energy and make yourself tired early in the ride. By relying on all three support points, you distribute the load and avoid tiring one body part too soon, especially on a weeklong tour, where you want to avoid exhausting one area in the first few days. To lessen the load on your butt on a long tour, lightly float your rear over the saddle, barely touching the seat, without much downward pressure. Use the saddle more as a guide to locate and control the bike. Also, when obstacles kick the bike up, you won't get knocked around as much, and you'll be able to react quicker and flick your bike and body around faster.

Bunny-hop. To fly over small obstacles such as roots or logs less than 6 inches high, use the bunny-hop. A bonus to learning this mountain bike move: You can also use it on the road to hop over potholes or cracks in the road. About two bike lengths before the obstacle you want to hop, level the pedals with your dominant foot forward. Having your stronger foot forward will help keep you from yanking the bike sideways while you're in the air. Next, flex your elbows and bend your knees as you crouch down over the bike. Your weight should be centered and you should maintain a straight line, which will help prevent you from sliding out on the landing. About a wheel length before the obstacle, press down with your arms, which will compress the suspension fork, then pull up on the bar while also pulling up with your feet. (Think of your feet as bird's claws pulling the pedals from the bottom up. With clipless pedals, this pulling up is easier.)

Roll over logs. Big log? No problem. Even logs larger than 6 inches high—so tall that your chainring will hit them—can be conquered with the following move: Set yourself up so that you're heading at the log perpendicularly. Then, about 6 feet before the log, stop pedaling in the 2 o'clock and 8 o'clock positions, with your stronger foot forward. Slightly bend your knees, stand, and coast with your toes pointed slightly down. Within a wheel length of the log, compress the front wheel by pushing down the handlebar with your arms, then pull up, drawing the bar to your chest. Lean forward as the chainring digs into the log. If you don't lean forward, your weight and momentum will be stuck on the back side of the log and you'll get caught up and fall to one side. As your weight shifts over the log and your torso leans forward, bend your knees as you sink into the bike. When the front wheel touches down on the other side of the log, begin pedaling and keep the bar in one line. Don't turn the bar while going over the log, or you'll slide out. As the rear wheel rolls over the log, shove the bike forward and shift your weight back slightly to the rear, just behind your pedals.

Climb rocky hills. Here, traction is king, because if your rear wheel spins out, you'll probably have to hop off the bike. To increase rear-wheel traction, move your butt up on the saddle so the seat's nose is wedged between your cheeks. A bit uncomfortable, sure, but it'll stick the rear wheel into the ground to keep traction. Keep the front wheel down by leaning forward so your shoulders are above the bar. You'll probably spin slower than your normal cadence, and that's fine. Just concentrate on keeping your cadence steady. That way you'll avoid bouncing and losing traction. When you pedal, instead of pulling your knees up to your chest, drive them toward the bar. This keeps you from working against gravity and brings the force of your leg muscles up and away from the hill. As you spin, avoid clipping rocks with your pedals by temporarily stopping your pedal stroke or by ratcheting a pedal backward and then, when it's clear, forward. Scoot your hands to the outsides of the bar to increase your leverage as you weave through rocks and need to switch lines to prevent the front wheel from getting stuck. Stay relaxed by keeping your elbows flexed; this also allows you to more easily shift your body and the bike as you roll up the rocks.

Descend steep downhills. Approach the edge at a walking pace. Stand on leveled pedals, center your weight, put your elbows up and out, and bend in your knees slightly. As you drop in and pick up speed, shift your body way back and conform to the angle of the descent. The steeper the slope, the farther back you'll be. On the steepest slopes, the saddle will even tap your chest while your butt floats over the rear tire. Look forward and keep your arms straight, with your elbows loose and your knees bent. With your weight back, you can use the front brake more to control your speed, since too much braking with the rear can cause you to skid and lose control. Brake more on smooth sections and let the bike roll over the rough stuff. As you roll out, carry your speed, and if it's a sharp landing, pull up on the bar to take the weight off the front wheel.

Push your bike. Put your body on the left side of the bike. That way your legs won't get caught in the drivetrain and you'll avoid getting chain gunk on your leg or clothes. It's also easier to get back on from

---

WHAT TO DO WHEN OFF THE BIKE

Push on gradual climbs that are too technical or long to ride.
Carry on steep grades when your feet begin to slip.

---

the left; and if you have to carry your bike, it's easier to heft it on your shoulder, again avoiding the drivetrain. Put your left hand on the bar and brake to steer and to be ready to lift the bike over obstacles. Also, with your fingers on the brake lever, you can grab the brake to help you stop if you slip. With your right hand, instead of grabbing the other handlebar, hold the top tube. This provides more support and steadiness, and you can also better guide the rear of the bike and keep it from bouncing. As you're pushing your bike, angle it slightly toward you. The top tube should be about a forearm's distance from your torso, and the wheels should be 3 to 6 inches farther away. This angle gives your legs more room to move without catching the pedal or other parts of the bike. Level the pedals so they'll have less chance of catching on rocks or roots.

Roll up and down switchbacks. Off-road terrain features that you won't find on the road include tight switchbacks. Often, these are strewn with rocks and roots and are lots steeper than the surrounding trail. To go up a switchback, prepare by taking a few deep breaths and clicking into a gear that's slightly harder than you'd pick if the rise were a straight climb—say, small chainring/third-from-largest cog. This allows you to power up the hill, increases traction, and decreases the number of pedal strokes it takes to roll up. Lean forward, and keep your elbows flexed through the switchback to avoid tensing up and stalling out. Follow the wide line to the outside of the turn; this is where the traction will be better and the trail less steep. Look at the line you'll take through the turn, and as you plan for the smoothest route, figure on your rear wheel tracking to the inside of the front by as much as a foot. That means the rock you dodge with the front may hang up your rear tire. To help steer the rear of the bike, swivel your hips on the saddle. Start with your weight on the inside of the turn, then swing out and back. On a right-hand turn, your hips will trace a letter C as they move. As you pass the apex of the turn, dip your inside shoulder a little and slide your butt forward on the saddle, but don't stand.

Going down a switchback, apply both brakes hard about 15 feet before the turn. Enter the switchback at a speed you can maintain the whole time. If you overestimate, scrub speed by feathering the rear brake. Don't touch the front while in the turn. Center your weight over the bike and keep the outside pedal down as you put about 80 percent of your weight on it. Roll along the outside arc of the turn. At the apex, slow slightly with the rear brake, and angle your bar to the inside of the turn so that your front wheel points straight out the exit. Release the brake and roll on.

Deal with mud, water, and sand. If you know you might be going into wet conditions, have a garbage bag handy for storing your soiled stuff after the ride. Also keep extra clothes around, along with towels for wiping down.

Mud on trails is inevitable. Some trails, like those in the Pacific Northwest, are perpetually wet and can still be ridden because the soil soaks up the water. Where rain is less frequent, avoid riding on wet trails; failure to heed this advice can damage the trail and the surrounding environment. When you do encounter the occasional puddle, it's better to ride through it, not around it, otherwise you'll widen the spot.

In thick or deep mud, shift gears earlier than usual to reduce stress on the drivetrain. Keep your cadence fairly high—75 to 85 rpm—to reduce your chance of stalling and to make it easier to maintain a spin as you roll through the muck. Keep your weight a little farther back on the bike than normal. To keep the front wheel from diving in the goo, you may need to yank up on the bar.

RIDE WITH AN ENVIRONMENTAL CONSCIOUSNESS

The International Mountain Bicycling Association (IMBA), an advocacy organization that also provides information about trails around the world, offers these 10 guidelines for low-impact riding that will make your riding safer and preserve the trails for others. For more information, visit www.imba.com.

1. Be prepared. Know your equipment, your ability, the weather, and the area you are riding, and prepare accordingly. A well-planned ride will go smoothly for you and your companions.

2. Don't ride on closed trails. A closed trail is off-limits for a reason, whether to protect the environment or for rider safety. Riding closed trails is not only illegal, it gives mountain bikers a bad reputation.

3. Say no to mud. Riding a muddy trail can cause unnecessary trail widening and erosion that may lead to long-lasting damage.

4. Respect the trail, wildlife, and environment. Be sensitive to the trail and its surroundings by riding softly and never skidding. Do not litter, and never scare animals.

Don't ride through water that would submerge your hubs, because you don't want the grease to wash away from the bearings. Once water gets stuck in there, it's a whole lotta trouble to get it out. So especially if you're on a long tour and away from a shop or tools that can help, it's a good idea to keep hubs dry.

Sometimes trails have sections of sand. If you're unready for it, you'll wash out or get stuck. First, put 60 to 80 percent of your weight back, because the front wheel needs to lightly float above the surface instead of digging in. Click into a gear that's one or two harder than you'd ride normally. It'll help you sit back on the saddle. Steer with

5. Stay on the trail. Do not intentionally ride off trail. Never cut switchbacks. Doing either can damage the ecosystem.

6. Ride slowly on crowded trails. Just as on a busy highway, when trails are crowded, you must move slowly to ensure safety for all trail users.

7. Pass with courtesy and care. Slow down when approaching other trail users, and respectfully make others aware that you are approaching. Pass with care, and be prepared to stop if necessary.

8. Share the trail with other trail users. Mountain bikers, hikers, and equestrians must share multiuse trails. Remember: Mountain bikers should yield to hikers and equestrians.

9. Don't do unauthorized trailwork. Moving logs or trimming trees may seem like a good idea, but those obstacles may actually serve functions such as moving water off the trail. Performing unauthorized and possibly illegal trailwork may lead to environmental damage, injury, or even potential trail closure.

10. Get involved. If you want to make a difference in your mountain biking community, get involved with a local club. Visit www.imba.com to find a club in your area.

your body and rely less on turning the handlebar and braking. Use exaggerated body English to direct your bike. For example, to make a right-hand turn on sand, countersteer by flicking the bar to the left. This will make your front wheel act like a rudder, swinging the rear wheel out and setting most of your weight in the direction of the turn.

Roll over roots. If you know you'll be riding over lots and lots of roots, lower your mountain bike's tire pressure to about 40 psi. This will provide traction and a good cushion. Roots perpendicular to the trail are no problem. A little lift on the front wheel and you're over. The thing is, roots are rarely perpendicular to the trail. So what to do on the many occasions when they're not? First, never brake on roots; doing so makes you more likely to slip and also drains the momentum that would help you roll over. Enter the root section with enough speed to clear the obstacles without pedaling hard. Cranking down on your pedals over roots will cause your wheels to slip. On uphills, accelerate as you approach, then lift the front wheel just enough to clear the root. Then lunge forward and unweight the rear wheel. You can soft-pedal to help the rear wheel over if needed. On downhills, stop pedaling, level your pedals, and balance your weight between your hands and feet. Float your butt just above the saddle. Raise the front wheel over the roots and let it just barely skim them. As the rear wheel rolls over, unweight it and stay light and centered on your wheels so you can flutter across. If a wheel slips, stay with it instead of jumping off the bike. A little more forward motion may do the trick to keep you upright.

Fly over drop-offs. These are ledges that may sneak up on you as you're riding down a trail. But you can roll through even 2-foot-deep drops by following a few simple tips. As the front wheel passes the ledge, lift while standing on leveled pedals. Pull up the front wheel enough that it's level with the rear. Shift your weight slightly back, and look through the landing area, about 10 feet ahead of you. As the rear wheel goes over the ledge, bring the bike closer to your body by bending your knees and pulling up on the pedals. Just before you land, slightly extend your arms and legs. This helps ease the bike to the ground and gives you the flexibility to absorb the impact of landing. Touch both wheels down at the same time. Bend at the elbows and knees as the bike hits the ground, and let your butt drop behind the seat to soak up the shock.

CHAPTER 7

Training

Begin your first fitness plan or fine-tune your engine
with these time-tested workouts

There's a somewhat unfair but wholly true formula for training and cycling: The better you train, the more fun you'll have. Don't let that discourage you, though. Even if you haven't ridden a bike in years, you
can still have a fantastic tour experience because the bike is, after all,
the amazing invention that makes more efficient use of human power
than any other machine. Friendly, easy-to-pedal gears make climbing
hard hills easy as long as you're in no rush; and on supported tours, a
van mercifully loaded with snacks usually brings up the rear to scoop
you up if you want to call it a day.

On the hard-core extreme, being physically prepared means that you
can challenge the monster climbs of the Tour de France and that you
have the juice to mountain bike to the most remote parts of the world.
When you're moderately fit, you won't be afraid to sign up for side
trips, and you can easily tack on extra miles to a loop. And if you have
just a bit of saddle time before a casual tour, you're less likely to have
sore private parts. That alone should get you spinning.

In this chapter, you'll find simple, easy-to-follow plans for getting
into shape in a short time. You'll learn how to prime your bod for fast,
tough tours and how to survive riding 100 miles in a day. There's even
a sample log on page 128 for charting your training progress and, on
page 118, tips that will make your tour easier even if you have had only
minimal training. So pick the plan that fits your needs, then hit the road.

TRAIN TO CARRY A LOAD

Once your bike is loaded with fenders, racks, panniers, a trailer, and whatever else you take to haul around your stuff, all that extra weight will change its stability and handling—which means your riding techniques must also change, as outlined in chapter 5. Whatever your experience level, you should make sure your training includes *at least* two rides in which your bike is loaded with the same equipment you'll have with you on tour. If possible, one of your fully loaded rides should be a longer weekend ride.

A loaded bike may change your climbing style, the way you pedal on flats, and how you control your bike on descents. Going uphill, you won't be able to stand and sway the bike from side to side. On flats, it'll be harder to maintain a high cadence. And going downhill, your bike may pull in different ways. So during training you should concentrate more on sitting and spinning in the low, easy gears. Use all parts of your pedal stroke, with power to the pedals as you push down *and* as you pull up on every stroke. If you only mash the pedals, you're only using half of your muscles.

Here are three workouts to hone your pedal stroke.

Perfect circles. Pedal through the 6 o'clock position as though

---

GET FIT ON THE SLY

Commuting to work is a great way to get into shape for a tour, and rack up some training miles. Plus, you'll be riding in weather that may not be so nice, just as on your tour. Here are some hints to make commuting easier. Early in the week, drive to work with your bike, a change of clothes, and some baby wipes to help you freshen up after your ride in if there's no shower at work. Then ride home that afternoon and back to work the next day.

---

pulling your foot back to scrape mud off the bottom of your shoe. Begin the pull-scraping motion at 3 o'clock. To get through the 12 o'clock dead spot, pedal as if you were standing on a barrel and pushing it with your feet: Start the pressure at 10 o'clock and keep rolling over the top until you hit 3 o'clock.

Low-gear downhills. On a descent, select a low gear that offers slight resistance as you increase your cadence to between 130 and 150 rpm. Try to avoid bouncing in the saddle and rocking your hips. This boosts the quality of your pedal stroke by helping your muscles learn to pedal through the critical dead spots at the top and bottom of each stroke. Rapid pedaling leads to greater efficiency, fluid leg motion, and more power to the drivetrain.

Granny-gear sprints. These are similar to low-gear downhills, except they're done on flat roads. Shift to your lowest gear, increase your cadence to between 130 and 150 rpm, and sprint for 20 to 30 seconds.

Over the first few days of a fully loaded tour, you can count on a loaded bike slowing your normal pace by 3 to 4 mph. You'll get some speed back as your legs get used to the weight. Until then, here's a good way to compensate: Schedule light mileage during your first week of a long, loaded tour and increase the mileage over the days. What's more important than mileage or speed is being able to maintain a solid cadence between 75 and 95 rpm.

To determine if you're hitting the target rpm, have a watch handy and count the number of full strokes you make during 30 seconds. Double that number and that's your rpm.

It takes more arms, abs, and back muscles to control a loaded bike while cornering, especially if the weight is over the rear wheel. You'll also need upper-body strength to keep the bike under control on long, winding descents. One cycling-specific way to boost these muscles is to ride a mountain bike once a week. Off the bike, you can do pushups, pullups, and crunches. Two or three times a week, do two or three sets of 10 to 15 repetitions.

Pushup

Support your body with your toes and hands, positioning the latter slightly wider than shoulder-width apart, palms flat on the floor. Straighten your arms without locking your elbows.

Lower your torso until your chest is just a fraction of an inch above the floor. Push yourself back to the starting position.

Pullup

Grab a chinning bar with an overhand grip that's slightly wider than shoulder width, and hang with your elbows slightly bent.

Pull your chin above the bar, hold for a second or two, then slowly lower yourself.

Crunch

Lie with your knees bent and your feet flat on the floor, as shown above. Once comfortable, fold your arms across your chest or hold your hands behind your ears. (Don't interlock your fingers behind your head or neck.)

Use your abs to lift your head and upper torso while keeping your lower back pressed firmly against the floor. Pause with your shoulder blades a few inches off the floor, then slowly return to the starting position.

HOW MUCH SHOULD YOU TRAIN?

Supported touring. You'll be fine if you can work up to rides that are two-thirds the length of your average daily trip mileage. That means if you'll be averaging 35 miles a day, you should be able to comfortably ride about 23 miles beforehand. Use the beginner plan below.

Self-supported. You'll probably be okay if you ride three or four times a week for 6 to 8 weeks, gradually increasing mileage. Speed isn't as important as getting your body used to spending lots of time in the saddle. Check out the intermediate plan on page 116.

Century rides. Ramp up your mileage so that you'll have at least one ride of 75 miles before expecting to ride 100 miles in 1 day. You'll have to increase your weekly mileage as well as the length and intensity of some of your rides. The intermediate plan on page 116 takes you there.

Hard-core touring. If you're planning on tackling some of the famous Tour de France climbs or a way-out-there mountain bike trip, you need to be in the best shape possible. Some touring companies may provide specific training plans, but the advanced plan on page 120 will get just about anyone ready for any trip.

BEGINNER TRAINING

This plan is for riders who . . .

• Haven't ridden much or at all recently

• Need to step up fitness for a relaxed-pace tour

TEST YOUR TOUR FITNESS

Think you're ready for your tour? To see if you're fit enough, figure out the daily average mileage and see if you can ride that far two or three times a week. If not, it's definitely time for one of our training plans.

- Want to keep training simple

- Don't have much time to train

If you haven't been riding much or at all, start here. It doesn't matter what shape you're in; the easy-to-follow 8-week plan at right is designed for time-crunched recreational riders who want to improve endurance for a relaxed-pace tour. In addition to helping you ride your tour with confidence, this plan will get your butt used to time in the saddle and improve your fitness so you can enjoy cycling at home and hang with the pack on group rides.

As you're preparing for your tour, the following tips will help build endurance, strength, and skills.

Double up on water. Most people don't drink enough water in the first place. Sweating while riding means it's even more important to stay hydrated. A good rule of thumb for starting out is to double your intake. Two quick ways to tell if you're sipping enough H_2O: You have to get up every night to go to the bathroom, and your pee is clear, not yellow.

Train for terrain. After about 3 weeks, add some terrain to your training that mimics what you'll be riding on your tour. For example, if there's a long climb or a day with a lot of descending, add a loop that has similar features and ride it once a week.

Notch two-thirds. To build your confidence and ensure you'll ride without suffering, be sure you get in a ride that's two-thirds of your average daily mileage at least once. Then, taper your mileage and intensity during the final week of training.

De-stress rides. Get in the habit of laying out your clothes and other gear the night before you ride. Starting a ride stressed out from scrambling around your house for gloves is a bad way to begin and will take your attention from the road. Also, fill your water bottles and check the pressure in your tires the night before.

Stretch. Another good habit to develop on training rides is stretching about every 30 minutes. Stand on the pedals and arch your back. Flex

8-WEEK BEGINNER TRAINING PLAN

	Mon.	Tues.	Wed.	Thurs.	Fri.	Sat.	Sun.	WEEKLY MILEAGE
Intensity	Pace	Optional	Pace	Off	Brisk	Pace	Pace	
Week 1	5	Optional	7	Off	9	20	15	56
Week 2	10	Optional	10	Off	10	25	18	73
Week 3	11	Optional	11	Off	11	30	20	83
Week 4	12	Optional	12	Off	12	35	22	93
Week 5	13	Optional	13	Off	13	40	24	103
Week 6	14	Optional	14	Off	14	45	29	116
Week 7	15	Optional	15	Off	15	50	34	129
Week 8 (week before tour)	10 easy	Optional	10	Off	10	30	5 easy	65

Optional = Rest or go for an easy spin of not more than 10 miles
Easy = You'll barely break a sweat, but keep your cadence high while riding 10 to 12 mph, or about 5 mph slower than your tour pace
Pace = The speed you want to maintain during your tour. A good goal: 12 to 14 mph
Brisk = 2 to 5 mph faster than you plan to ride your tour

your ankles down to stretch your calves. Shrug your shoulders and bend your neck from side to side and down and up. This will prevent fatigue.

Draft. One of the best ways to conserve energy, especially over long touring days in the saddle, is to draft. Pro cyclists (and even NASCAR drivers) use this technique all the time: They tuck in behind an opponent and allow the rider or driver in front to expend extra energy parting the wind. When you draft, you can save up to 40 percent of your energy. Think about how much you'll save if you catch such a slipstream for just 2 hours of a long ride.

To get the most benefit from drafting, you should be between 6 inches and 1 foot from the wheel in front of you. On training rides with

(continued on page 115)

HOW TO SAVE YOUR BUTT (AND A FEW OTHER IMPORTANT PARTS)

Even if you're picking up this book just days before your first tour, leaving yourself no time for a formal training program, we have some tips that can save you a buttload (literally) of pain.

Since saddle sores can ruin your trip, you want to stop the hot spots before they stop you. Here's how.

Balm your butt. Friction causes these butt busters. Rub A&D ointment with zinc oxide on your chamois and skin. It'll decrease friction and keep your skin lubricated. Another option some cyclists swear by: Bag Balm, an ointment farmers use to soothe cows' dry teats.

Scrub with soap and warm water. Before and after riding, thoroughly wash to reduce the bacteria in your shorts.

Regularly wash your shorts. Bacteria breed in warm, damp places such as cycling shorts. Even if your shorts are dry, don't wear them again without washing them first. For a tour of a week or less, women especially might want to pack a fresh pair of shorts for each day.

Let your body breathe. Do a little streaking after a ride to air out all your naughty bits, then change into dry, baggy shorts.

Check your saddle. A saddle that's loose or too high can create friction that causes saddle sores. If the nose is tilted too far up or down, that can also cause sores. The saddle should be level.

Ditch gel covers. Those saddle pads that seem like a good, comfy idea at first can cause butt troubles later. The gel conforms to your buttocks and shifts up into places a saddle shouldn't go, causing friction. If you want more comfort, get a more padded chamois.

Right after the bottom area, the second most common source of pain is the wrists. The following tips will solve many hand ailments.

Change hand positions. This is easier on a road bike, where you can place your hands on different parts of the bar, such as the top of the bar, the hoods, the drops, and where the bar curves forward. A good rule of thumb: Change hand position about every 10 minutes.

Pump 'em up. Get stronger wrists with reverse wrist curls: Hold a barbell with an overhand grip, kneel alongside a bench, and rest your forearms on the bench with your hands hanging off the other side. Bend your wrists to lower the weight toward the floor. Then lift the weight as high as you can without moving your forearms. Do three sets of 10 to 12 reps, two or three times a week.

(continued on page 114)

Reverse wrist curl

HOW TO SAVE YOUR BUTT—*CONTINUED*

Stretch to the shoulder

"Perp" stretch

Especially if you have not ridden much lately, your neck will be sore from craning forward on the bike. Doing the following two stretches every day (or every ride) will make your neck more flexible and will ward off pain.

Stretch to the shoulder. Sit or stand up straight and look forward. Reach over your head with your left hand and put it on the right side of your head. Gently bring your left ear toward your left shoulder. Hold for 30 to 60 seconds. Switch sides and repeat.

Strike a "perp" pose. Sit or stand up straight and look forward. Put both hands behind your head with fingers interlaced. Spend 10 seconds pushing your head against your hands and your hands against your head. Relax and repeat the stretch 3 to 5 times.

others, you can get comfortable drafting by slowly riding closer to a more experienced cyclist. Always let the other rider know you're there by asking if you may draft or at least giving a head nod. Avoid touching your brakes while drafting. Instead, to adjust your position, sit up and let your body catch more wind. Also, don't fixate on the wheel of the rider in front of you. Shift your gaze between the wheel and the road 30 to 50 feet ahead.

Avoid These Five Common Beginner Mistakes

1. Just noodling around. Even on the beginner training plan, your time in the saddle won't be as beneficial if you don't follow the recommended pace and schedule. On rest days, rest; on brisk days, don't slack off. A good way to stick to the plan is to do it with a friend—that way, you'll feel obligated and you'll nudge each other to put in the miles.

2. Not eating enough on the bike. On rides longer than 2 hours, you should eat a small snack about every 30 minutes. Two good choices: half an energy bar or a banana. And drink plenty of water while eating—sip about a bottle of water per hour.

3. Skipping days, then quitting. Of course, you can't ride every single mile of every workout day. Here and there you'll miss a day; other days you'll be pressed for time and unable to finish all the miles. Don't let these lapses become a rationale for quitting altogether. Instead, pick up the next day's schedule when you can and keep on riding. You'll still reap the benefits come tour time.

4. Gasping and losing breath. We naturally breathe rhythmically, with exhalations coming on downstrokes. If you consciously break that rhythm, you'll eliminate energy-wasting gasps on climbs or during fast periods of riding. Do an extralong exhalation every 10 pedal strokes.

5. Starting cold, stopping hot. Especially if your day's scheduled training is a harder, brisk ride, allow about 30 minutes of easy spinning to warm up. This primes your muscles for the effort and helps prevent injuries. Then, when you finish your workout, don't just hop off your bike. Allow about 10 minutes to cool down as you lightly spin.

INTERMEDIATE TRAINING

This plan is for riders who . . .

- Plan to ride solo or longer tours

- Already ride more than 50 miles a week and are ready for more

- Can devote 6 to 10 hours a week to training

- Are comfortable on group rides

This plan is based on *Bicycling* magazine's 10-week century training plan that approximately 1 million cyclists have used to successfully ride 100 miles in 1 day. For a solo cyclist, knowing you've got that kind

10-WEEK INTERMEDIATE TRAINING PLAN

	Mon.	Tues.	Wed.	Thurs.	Fri.	Sat.	Sun.	WEEKLY MILEAGE
Intensity	Easy	Pace	Brisk	Rest	Pace	Pace	Pace	
Week 1	6	10	12	Rest	10	30	9	77
Week 2	7	11	13	Rest	11	34	10	86
Week 3	8	13	15	Rest	13	38	11	98
Week 4	8	14	17	Rest	14	42	13	108
Week 5	9	15	19	Rest	15	47	14	119
Week 6	11	15	21	Rest	15	53	16	131
Week 7	12	15	24	Rest	15	59	18	143
Week 8	13	15	25	Rest	15	65	20	153
Week 9	15	15	25	Rest	15	65	20	155
Week 10	15	15	25	Rest	10	5 easy	100	170

Easy = About 5 mph slower than your typical ride pace
Pace = The speed you want to maintain during your tour, about 14 to 18 mph for an intermediate rider
Brisk = 2 to 5 mph faster than your usual pace

of mileage in your legs makes the difference between reaching the campground before dark and having to sneak a tent onto Farmer Johnson's back 40. The best thing about this plan is that if you miss a day, you can simply resume the schedule the next time you can get back in the saddle.

Stick close to the plan and follow these tips, and you'll ride strong on just about any tour—for sure.

Don't just ride. You won't build muscles or speed recovery if you don't go hard when you should go hard and easy when you should go easy. When you start the 10-week training plan, stick to the prescribed miles *and* intensity for each day.

Buddy up. Make at least one of your weekend rides with a group. Even better: Ride with your spouse or friends who are also planning to go along on the tour. This will make you comfortable riding in a group and a paceline, which will help conserve energy.

Eat with purpose. Eat within 30 minutes after every training ride. During this half-hour window, your body is primed to absorb and replace glycogen—the fuel that pumps your muscles. Add more protein to your diet by eating a mix of about 60 percent carbs, 20 percent fat, and 20 percent protein. Two tasty examples: turkey on whole wheat, or pasta with red sauce and a few sprinkles of Parmesan.

Spin, spin, spin. Many riders who want to build endurance spin too slowly. While training and during your tour, shoot for a cadence of 90 to 100 rpm. For most types of riding, this cadence is the most efficient and helps decrease damage to knees and tendons.

Sleep tight. Get 8 hours of shut-eye a night. If you keep staying up to watch Dave's Top Ten List, you might get a good chuckle, but you'll impair motor skills, judgment, reflexes, memory, and concentration.

Five Tips for Long, Nasty Rides

When riding for 50 miles or more, whether training or touring, use the following strategies to stay strong.

FIVE TIPS FOR RIDING
LONG DISTANCES IN 1 DAY

Without a strategy for your long ride, you'll suffer, or worse, maybe not finish. These tips will help you go the distance on just about any day of touring.

1. Load those carbs. Two days before you hit the road, belly up to the carb bar. For breakfast, eat whole grain cereals such as Total or Cracklin' Oak Bran. For lunch and dinner, go for pastas, brown rice, beans, or other carb-heavy meals that you have had before and that are easy on your stomach.

2. Take 'er easy. To begin your day, click into an easy gear to warm up your muscles. Don't get caught up in the initial rush. Find a pace that's good for you. If possible, hook up with two or three other riders who are at your same pace and take turns pulling in a paceline. It's a great way to take breaks, and drafting behind another rider can save up to 40 percent of your energy.

3. Break it up. Don't start your long touring or century with that

---

Split it. Plan on riding faster the second half of your day than the first. The first 5 to 10 miles should be at about 70 percent of your max heart rate. (See "Be Heart Smart" on page 122.) Once you pass the halfway mark, boost your effort.

Fuel fast. Even on leisurely, long rides your body consumes about 4,000 calories and burns about 50 percent carbs and 50 percent fat. To stoke your inner fire, squeeze back an energy gel about every 45 minutes and drink a bottle of energy drink about every hour.

Play the group. Instead of just getting by in a group of riders, you want to get in the front as soon as possible and hop in a fast paceline. Out front, you'll be with other fast riders who can help you save energy and pick up the tempo. When you're in a paceline, stay at least big end-of-the-day goal looming in your head. Instead, break the ride into parts. Think of it in segments, such as from one rest stop to another, or four 25-mile increments. It's less intimidating, and when you reach each milestone, you'll feel like you've accomplished something.

4. Make quick pit stops. Don't rest for more than 10 minutes at a time. If you're standing around stuffing your face, your legs will also cool and stiffen. Instead, pack some snacks you can eat every 30 minutes on the bike. Go for foods loaded with carbs and protein, such as turkey subs, PB&J, fig bars, hummus wraps, and bagel sandwiches.

5. Dodge the wall. Somewhere around the 60-mile mark, lots of cyclists get mentally and physically tired. The end still seems far off. Fortunately, the solution tastes really good: Eat a Snickers bar. The combination of chocolate, peanuts, and other sweet stuff will give you a kick. Plus, it's a reward for getting that far. Get one from a rest stop, or freeze one and take it along.

6 inches behind the rider in front of you to get the most benefit from the draft.

Don't cross your lactate threshold. Don't go anaerobic. Once you force your metabolism to switch—even briefly—from aerobic to anaerobic energy production, you may not recover for the rest of the ride. So don't pull hard on steep climbs or in strong headwinds.

Finish strong. Dip down to your reserves, take another swig of energy drink, and kick in the afterburners in the last 15 miles. You'll get a kick of adrenaline when you know that you're nearing the end. Take advantage of it by picking up the pace. And once you finish, thank your muscles by stretching out and eating a big meal loaded with carbs.

ADVANCED TRAINING

This plan is for riders who . . .

- Already average more than 75 miles a week

- Have 12 to 18 hours a week to train

- Can supplement riding with gym work

- Have good group riding skills

You don't want to merely survive long, hard rides. You want to thrive. You want to ride with the toughest of the tough and enter elite cycling circles, ride the same roads the pros suffer on, and maybe even crank out a 5-hour century. Just follow the 10-week, high-octane training plan on the opposite page, and you'll build your speed slowly and surely for a load of power and endurance come tour time. In addition to enabling you to go longer and stronger, this training plan and the following tips will get you ready to tackle even the most mountainous roads.

Add intervals. Once a week, after a warmup at 75 percent of your maximum heart rate, include short intervals at 90 to 95 percent of your maximum heart rate. (See "Be Heart Smart" on page 122.) As you get closer to your tour and become more fit, your heart rate will rise more slowly and fall more quickly. That means you'll be able to go longer stronger.

Hit the hills. Pick one or two weeks during the training plan to specifically work hills. Work on technique by pushing down with your heels and sliding back on your seat to use your hamstrings to power you up. Use your quads to pull up on the pedals as you slide forward on the seat.

Avoid overtraining. Of course you're going to miss a training day here and there; don't make up for it by going overboard and adding more miles or over-the-top intensity. The 10-week plan allows plenty of time to make up for a few skipped days. Pick up where you left off

10-WEEK ADVANCED TRAINING PLAN

	Mon.	Tues.	Wed.	Thurs.	Fri.	Sat.	Sun.	WEEKLY MILEAGE
Intensity	Pace	Optional	Pace	Off	Brisk	Pace	Pace	
Week 1	10	12	14	Rest	12	40	15	10
Week 2	10	13	13	Rest	13	44	17	110
Week 3	10	15	17	Rest	15	48	18	123
Week 4	11	16	19	Rest	16	53	20	135
Week 5	12	18	20	Rest	18	59	22	149
Week 6	13	19	23	Rest	19	64	24	162
Week 7	14	20	25	Rest	20	71	27	177
Week 8	16	20	27	Rest	20	75	29	187
Week 9	17	20	30	Rest	20	75	32	194
Week 10	19	20	30	Rest	10	5 easy	100	184

Easy = About 5 mph slower than your tour pace
Pace = The speed you want to maintain during the tour, about 18 to 25 mph
Brisk = 2 to 5 mph faster than your usual pace

and stick to it. And always rest: You don't get stronger from riding; you get stronger from resting.

Eat smart. All the training miles in the world won't do you any good if you stuff your face with pork rinds. Eat meals with 65 to 70 percent carbs, 20 to 25 percent fat, and 15 percent high-quality protein. Good foods include grilled chicken, baked fish, turkey, and lean grilled beef, along with side dishes of plenty of fruits and veggies and, of course, lots of water.

Strengthen your core. Hit the gym once or twice a week for about 30 minutes. Don't work on your legs; instead, beef up your abdominal and lower-back muscles. When these muscles are strong, you'll ward

BE HEART SMART

When riding, as with falling in love, you should listen to your heart. Strapping on a heart rate monitor can prevent you from pushing too hard, fatiguing, and burning out muscles instead of building them up. "No pain, no gain" is a myth.

Most of the time during training, you want to maintain a heart rate that's below your lactate threshold, the point where your body can no longer meet its demand for oxygen and starts producing lactic acid. You've reached your lactate threshold when your muscles start that intense burning. Elite athletes often train at a heart rate that'll keep them at about 85 percent of their lactate threshold. If you're in the area of 70 to 80 percent of your max, you're in a good zone that'll prevent fatigue and still build muscle.

How do you find your lactate threshold heart rate? There's an often-quoted but inaccurate formula for figuring this out: 220 minus your age. Ditch that. A better way to gauge your lactate threshold is to ride with a heart rate monitor. After about a 30-minute warmup, push yourself to the point where you're breathing hard and unable to carry on a conversation. Note your heart rate. Do this for three rides and take the average of those three heart rates. That's your max. Do a little math to back off that number by about 20 percent, and you'll find your ideal training rate. For example, if your max average is 210, then you should ride consistently at about 168.

off fatigue and avoid a sore back after notching even 100 fast miles. Some good ab and back exercises include the crunch (see page 108), reverse crunch, Russian twist, vacuum, and superman. For each of these, do two or three sets of 8 to 10 repetitions of each exercise, three times a week.

Reverse Crunch

Lie faceup with your arms at your sides. Hold your legs off the floor, with your knees bent at a 90-degree angle so your thighs point straight up and your lower legs point straight ahead, parallel to the floor.

Crunch your pelvis toward your rib cage. Your tailbone should rise a few inches off the floor as your knees move toward your chin. Pause, then slowly return to the starting position.

Russian Twist

Sit with your torso at a 45- to 60-degree angle to the floor (as if you're halfway through a situp) and your arms stretched directly out in front of you. Bend your knees and keep your feet free, not anchored by anything.

While maintaining this torso angle, rotate as far as possible to one side, and then, without pausing, to the other.

Vacuum

Get down on your hands and knees, keeping your back flat. Take a deep breath, allowing your belly to pouch out.

Forcibly exhale and round your back like an angry cat as you lift your navel up toward your spine. When you can exhale no more, keep your back rounded and your navel in as you purse your lips and take shallow breaths through your nose for several seconds. That's 1 rep; it should take 20 to 30 seconds. Inhale as you flatten your back to the starting position.

Superman

Lie facedown with your legs straight and your arms stretched in front of you, with your hands on the floor. Lift your arms, head, chest, and lower legs off the floor simultaneously. Hold this position for 1 to 5 seconds, keeping your head and neck at the same height as your shoulders throughout the movement.

WEEKLY TRAINING LOG

In addition to being a guide to becoming a better cyclist, your training log can help you preserve memories of specific rides and people you rode with. Make photocopies of the sample log page, staple them together or collect 'em in a binder, and keep them where you store your bike. That way, your log will be handy as you begin and finish rides.

Here's the information you should record.

Time. Note either the times you left for the ride and returned or the total amount of time spent riding. This will allow you to determine if there are times of day that are better for you to ride. Also, you'll see progress as you take longer and longer rides.

Distance. How many miles you rode. When following a training plan, you'll likely see an amazing increase in the number of miles from week to week and month to month.

Average speed. This is a measure of ride intensity. Sometimes a

PSYCH UP FOR ALL CONDITIONS

Cultivate a state of mind in which you're prepared for dreary weather, headwinds, changes of plans, and equipment failures. Figure out what kind of experience you're looking for and whether the people you're riding with share that idea. Will it be a pounding ride that is focused on the destination? Or will you stop at every vista for photos? Test the waters with a weekend or longer ride to see how your friends act; then you'll be ready.

short, fast ride can do you as much, if not more, good than a long, slow ride. If you don't have a computer that figures this, you can calculate it by dividing distance traveled by time taken. A little additional math may be needed to convert that total to mph, though. You'll need to divide distance by time. For example, a 42-mile ride divided by the 2.5 hours it took you means you rode an average of 16.8 mph.

Weather. By recording the weather conditions you train in, you can find out if you have a hard time in headwinds and compute how much slower you go in cold or rainy weather—invaluable knowledge when you're riding from campsite to campsite through storms.

Diet. What did you eat before and after the ride? By keeping this record, you'll find out what kinds of foods best fuel your efforts and which ones are better to avoid, especially before long rides. This is also a handy way to start watching the waistline.

Ride rating. On a scale of 1 to 10, with 10 being the best, rate how you felt during the ride. This will give you an indication of progress—as you start to ride longer or faster and still feel strong, you might want to stretch yourself more.

Postride rating. On a scale of 1 to 10, with 10 being the best, rate

(continued on page 130)

TRAINING LOG

WEEK ___	Time	Distance	Average Speed	Weather
SUN.				
MON.				
TUES.				
WED.				
THURS.				
FRI.				
SAT.				
TOTAL				X

	Diet	Ride Rating	Postride Rating	Other Notes
	X			X

how you feel about a half hour after the ride is over. This will give you an indication of how well you recover and clue you in to whether you need to add recovery supplements to your training.

Other notes. Include personal items such as top speed, whether you were with other riders and were drafting, if you had any mechanicals, or if a groundhog nearly ran you over.

Total. Add up your times and distances for the week. Lots of cyclists share this info at the coffee shop. Some even tell the truth.

CHAPTER 8

Eat and Drink

Smart

Get the fuel you need to ride strong

When you're on a cycling vacation, you're also on a break from dieting. And there's absolutely nothing wrong with that. On lots of bike tours, high-end, extravagant food is part of the allure. But you still have to eat right to ride. You are, after all, your own power plant, providing your transportation with your own legs.

When you plan your own trip, food is especially vital. You don't, after all, have a concierge to book restaurant reservations for you. Mess up your provisions, and you might wind up begging for candy bars.

Along with fueling your ride, you have to ensure that you have enough water. Getting it requires additional planning to carry it, find sources, or purify it.

So eat, drink, and indulge, sure, but this chapter's tips for eating on your bike and off will allow you to finish each day's ride—and your whole trip—feeling good.

FUEL UP

Starting a day's ride without eating anything is like expecting your car to run on fumes for miles and miles. When you sleep, you're fasting, so when you wake up, your energy stores (glycogen) are running low.

If you punt breakfast, your body will slow down even more. To replenish, eat a breakfast of about 400 calories 1½ to 2 hours before you start your day's ride. A good example is cereal with milk, 8 ounces of orange juice, and a bagel, plain or with a light spread of your favorite topping. Also drink three 8-ounce glasses of water.

During a ride, you have to replace carbohydrates that you burn. Eat about ½ gram of carbs per pound of body weight every hour. Drink 8 to 10 ounces of water with the food, especially with energy bars or gels, since those are low in water and will draw additional blood into your stomach to help absorb the food. Keeping your stomach fairly empty during the day will make you more comfortable, so instead of pulling up to the trough for one big midday meal, eat steadily throughout the day. Another downside to that large meal is that blood from elsewhere in the body will rush to the stomach to help absorb the meal. This robs your legs of oxygen and makes you more tired more quickly. Also, your stomach may get upset more easily if you resume riding while it's trying to finish digesting a large meal.

Don't make the mistake of thinking that sweet, sugary foods give you energy. Sure, you may get an initial boost because the sugar rapidly goes through your system and converts quickly to energy. But for longer efforts such as touring, riding the sugar roller coaster may be dangerous. A large amount of sugar in the bloodstream causes an increase in insulin to process the sugar. The sugar is quickly used as the insulin causes the body to store the excess. This rapid use and storage may actually leave you with low blood sugar levels and cause fatigue, headache, nausea, and potentially even blackouts.

On touring rides, you need an energy source that isn't burned as rapidly as sugar. Picking from a variety of food groups answers your needs. For a fully loaded touring cyclist, the additional weight may require the amount of energy equal to that used by a racing cyclist: 3,500 to 5,000 calories a day. Shoot for 65 to 70 percent of your calories from carbohydrates. Some good sources include beans, whole grain breads,

---

SMART SNACKS

Before a Ride

- Energy bars
- Bagels

- Sports drinks
- Bananas

- Energy gels

Midride

- Energy bars
- Raisins

- Sports drinks
- Wheat crackers

- Energy gels
- Animal crackers

After a Ride

- Bagel with peanut butter
- Wheat crackers

- Yogurt

---

and vegetables. These kinds of foods take longer to break down and become fuel, which makes them good for long-haul efforts. Take in 15 to 20 percent of your diet in fat, which you can get from low-fat dairy products such as yogurt and cheese. Make the remaining 15 to 20 percent of your diet protein. You can get protein from meats, such as chicken or beef. The protein helps you recover after long days in the saddle and rebuilds muscles.

For an all-day ride, a 150-pound cyclist needs about 75 grams of carbs to keep energy up. After 60 to 90 minutes of riding, it's a good idea to take a break and eat one of the following snacks: a 16-ounce sports drink and an energy bar; two energy gel packs of 50 grams and 12 ounces of a sports drink; a banana and four fig bars; a peanut butter and jelly sandwich on whole grain bread; a small bagel with 2 teaspoons of honey and 8 ounces of a sports drink. Another good idea:

NO-COOK GROCERY LIST

If your culinary ambitions are low and you're more of a grab-and-eat type of person, here's what you should—and shouldn't—pack along. Also, if you get the hankering for some warmed-up grub, one thing you can do is offer some of your supplies to someone who already has a fire going.

The Vittles	Pack-Friendly	Squishy Mess
Breads	Bagels, tortillas, baguettes, rolls	Loaf white
Cheeses	Monterey Jack, Cheddar	Brie
Fruits	Oranges, apples, raisins, pears	Bananas
Veggies	Carrots, cucumbers	Tomatoes, lettuce
Meats	Jerky, canned tuna	12-oz New York strip

Keep raw vegetables such as carrots, celery, bell peppers, and cauliflower within easy reach to munch on while you ride.

Within an hour after finishing a ride, eat. Go for carbs accompanied by protein. This will restore your muscle glycogen quickly and efficiently, making it easier for you to recover and ride strong the next day. A few examples of good postride meals include cereal with milk and bananas, turkey on whole grain bread, a peanut butter and jelly sandwich, a bagel with cream cheese, a slice of deep-dish pizza, yogurt with granola, and macaroni and cheese.

Your evening meal can be more substantial than the others you've had throughout the day. Load up on carbs. Look for whole grain pasta. Because pasta is easily portable and requires only water to prepare, it's a good choice. Plus, you can easily add variety to pasta by adding sauces, butter, or a mix of herbs.

DRINK LOTS

Shoot for drinking about a half bottle or 6 to 8 ounces of water every hour, taking sips about every 15 minutes. To help remember to drink as much as you should, sip every time you see another rider hitting the water bottle.

Whenever you have a chance to top off your water bottles, take it. Keeping a constant supply of water handy will help you avoid dehydration. The universal rule about H_2O: Drink *before* you're thirsty. If you wait until you're craving water, you may already be on the edge of dehydration. If you don't replace the water lost through sweating, your heart will beat faster but pump less blood, and your body temperature will increase, so your power output will plummet in as little as 30 minutes. Wait longer, and you're headed for heatstroke, hospital time, or worse.

Early signs of dehydration include headache, abnormal fatigue, and dizziness. You're near heatstroke if you vomit or stop sweating. If you experience any of these symptoms, stop riding and find some shade. Let your body rest, and wait at least 45 minutes before getting back on the bike—longer if you're riding in hot weather. You should also drink enough to make up for the water you should have been slugging. This may be one or two water bottles' worth, so drink up. If you can, drink cold fluids, because they're absorbed more quickly. Also, eat some fruits and vegetables, because they're 80 to 95 percent water. Nibble on a salty snack, too, because the sodium will make your blood sponge up more water.

Even if it's not hot outside, you need to keep sipping. On hotter days, you might need to drink as much as a gallon of water. The same is true if you're riding at high altitudes. You may think you don't need to drink much, because you may not notice sweat. As the air passes over your body, perspiration evaporates, so it may not seem like you're sweating it out. Keep drinking anyway.

POTENT POTABLES

	Filters	Iodine Tablets	Boiling	Bottled H$_2$O
Cost	♦♦ Good ones start at $50.	♦♦♦ They cost just $8 to $10.	♦♦♦♦ Got a match?	♦♦ Damn, it adds up.
Packability	♦♦ Less than a pound, and good ones wrap into their own small bags about as big as two spare tubes.	♦♦♦♦ Small bottles easily slip into your pocket.	♦ You're really gonna pack a pan on a ride?	♦♦ Climbs are killers when you're packing a few pounds of Perrier.
Ease of use	♦♦ If you can change a flat, you can assemble a filter and pump water through it.	♦♦♦ Some people can't get used to the taste.	♦ No way around it—it's a pain to boil for the minimum 3 minutes at a rolling boil.	♦ You don't wanna be searching for bottled water instead of riding.

♦ = Bad

♦♦ = Okay

♦♦♦ = Good

♦♦♦♦ = Best

To help wash down all this water and give it a little taste, you might want to squeeze some lemon into it. This tip will also help limit the amount of mucus buildup in your mouth.

When it's time to refill your water bottles, keep in mind some basic safety guidelines. Clear, standing water doesn't mean safe water. (If there's nothing living in the water, there's a reason for that.) Running water is better than still. The higher up a mountain you are, the safer the water. And outside the United States, soda and beer can be a safer bet than tap water.

To be sure that what you're sipping won't make you sick, you can purify water with a filter or iodine tablets, boil it, or buy the bottled kind. Many lightweight, easily portable filters are available, and they're often your best bet. Look for one with a charcoal core. For an ultra-lightweight option, tablets may be for you. "Potent Potables" examines the pluses and minuses of each method.

CHAPTER 9

Survive

Almost

Anything

Make like a Boy Scout and be prepared

Perhaps you've read the bestseller *The Worst-Case Scenario Survival Handbook*. Or maybe you tune in to *Survivor* every week. While nice and cozy in your comfy living room, you've probably wondered how you would manage to extricate yourself from similar bad situations. On a tour, such practical know-how can actually keep you rolling and prevent sticky situations like shivering under a bridge until the rain stops.

Because bike riding is such an eco-friendly activity, you might think Mother Nature would give cyclists a pass. No such luck. So it's better to be prepared than optimistic. Here are smart ways to be ready to ride into the worst stuff. Sure, you hope you won't have to use the following skills and tips. But you'll be glad you know 'em if tough situations come up. These are the kinds of pointers that help everyone from beginners to the most seasoned cyclists. And they take only a few minutes to learn.

RIDE THROUGH RAIN

There are two schools of thought about rainy rides: Cover up and protect, or embrace it and ride on wet. For shorter rides, it's okay to regale in a gentle shower. But having soggy equipment and clothes is no way to ride over a multiday tour.

The first trick to getting through the rain is to line everything, including your body. To shield yourself from the rain, one of the best cycling investments you can make is in a good, high-quality, waterproof jacket. Get one that's tailored for riding; it won't flop around or get in the way of pedaling or controlling the bike, as will other outerwear, such as ponchos or noncycling jackets. The best of these cycling jackets will have at least one type of zippered ventilation system or flaps to allow body heat to circulate out while you stay dry. Fabrics such as Gore-Tex and Activent are good. And while you might pay more than $100 for such a jacket, it'll last for years—and when the heavens open up, you'll be grateful for every penny spent. If it's a cold rain, some waterproof pants might be a good addition as well, but you may not like the additional weight on your legs as you're trying to pedal through the wet stuff.

To keep your vision clear, put Rain-X Original Glass Treatment on your glasses when you're packing and prepping your gear for your trip. It turns the raindrops into small beads that roll off your lenses. However, before putting Rain-X on plastic lenses, check with the glasses' manufacturer, since the product is designed for glass.

Also mount some mudguards on your bike to help keep you dry on wet roads and reduce the amount of water and grit that get in your brakes, drivetrain, and packs. Some models mount on the down tube and seatpost; others mount over the front and rear wheels like temporary fenders. Lightweight, plastic models are best; they don't rust and they can bend, if needed, to install. Mud flaps on the fenders will save any riding buddies from the spray.

If you'll be carrying panniers, look for ones made with weatherproof material such as Gore-Tex. In addition, you can line them with plastic bags and then take the further precaution of bagging everything you're packing within another set of plastic bags. Along with keeping equipment and food dry, this also allows you to more easily shift around weight from pannier to pannier to maintain balance.

If you can, avoid the most dangerous time to ride: the first 10 minutes after the rain starts (that's when the water picks up oils and carries them across the roadway). Take a 20- to 30-minute break to sit out that super-slippery time.

After a rainy ride, take a warm shower, if you can, and scrub down your private parts with a bar of antibacterial soap. In addition to feeling great, this washing will get rid of any bacteria that could cause saddle sores. All that water squishing around down there while you're riding can cause chafing. Once your butt is dry, do your bike a favor and spin the wheels to help get any remaining water out of the hub. Also, wipe down drivetrain components and areas around the headset. It'd also be a good time to drip on some additional lube so you'll be ready for the next day's ride.

BEAT THE HEAT

When planning your days of riding in hot weather, wake up early, in the predawn hours, and start riding with first light. This way, you'll be rolling during the coolest part of the day. A typical low-desert summer day, like the kind in California and Arizona and along the Colorado River valley, begins with a predawn temperature of usually no cooler than 75°F.

This predawn riding period is more valuable and short than you may think. After the sun is up, you can expect the temperature to jump about 10 degrees the first hour and 2 to 3 degrees per hour after that until the peak at about 1:00 P.M. With an average tolerance to heat, you can ride efficiently until 11:00 A.M. Plan on stopping about then and spending the afternoon near a water source and under some shade. Take the downtime as a chance to slug down water, have a decent meal, and rest. This is also a good opportunity to visit with locals, find the best homemade malts, or see the world's largest ball of aluminum foil.

(continued on page 144)

LIONS AND LIGHTNING AND BEARS— OH, MY!

Here are practical tips for managing seven dangers of the natural world.

Chased by dogs. You're not likely to outrun Fido, especially if you're carrying 30 pounds of equipment. The best strategy is to dismount and place your bike between you and the animal. Once you quit riding, dogs often decide that "the chase" is over and saunter back home. You can also yell "no," "stop," "heel," and other common pooch commands to end the pursuit. A few squirts of the water bottle may also make Cujo turn tail. If all else fails, try pepper spray.

Lightning. Bolts from above strike by height, so when a storm is brewing and you can't take cover inside, get as low as possible. But don't flop in a ditch; it will likely be filled with water, an excellent conductor of electricity. If your hair stands on end, immediately kneel or squat with your head between your knees. Kissing anything goodbye is entirely optional.

Snakebite. Stay away from slithering serpents, remembering that their striking range is about half the length of their bodies. Fortunately, few bites are fatal—and sometimes a poisonous snake doesn't even inject venom when it bites. However, if there's swelling and intense pain localized around the bite, it's a "hot" bite and you should seek help immediately. Mojave rattler and coral snakebites cause sleepiness, so you should keep the victim awake. In all cases, clean the wound with water and keep the victim hydrated until help arrives. Don't ice the bite, use a tourniquet, or cut the wound open and try to suck out venom.

Forest fire. Get to a safe area quick, because fire can move as fast as 30 mph on steep or fuel-rich terrain or in high winds. Look for an open field, a rock outcropping, or an area devoid of vegetation, including a stream or pond, which can be a safety zone away from the blaze. If surrounded by fire, clear the area around you of grasses, then make like a mole and burrow into the dirt. Don't flee into an unknown canyon—getting trapped in dead ends causes more outdoor fire-related deaths than anything else.

Mountain lion stare. When confronted with a mountain lion, maintain eye contact. Get off your bike and make yourself look tall: If you're wearing a jacket, unzip it and open the flaps to make yourself appear bigger. To try to scare or at least distract the big cat, throw items from your handlebar bag—tools, fruit, bagels, headlamp, journal, bike lock, whatever you've got in there. If attacked by a mountain lion, fight back using anything handy, including your bike or pump.

Tornado. There's no outpedaling a tornado, which moves at about 30 mph and can top 70 mph. Now, that's just how fast a twister covers distance. The wind speed inside can be more than 200 mph. In the woods, lie down in a ditch or gully. Cover your head and neck. Keep your helmet on, and if you're wearing a hydration pack, cover your neck with it. In more urban areas, find room for yourself and your bike in an interior closet or hallway on the lowest level of a building.

Bear attack. Avoid eye contact, and don't ride or run away. Hold your ground. If you're with others, huddle together. A bear has terrible eyesight, so it might mistake you for Andre the Giant or some other big creature that can beat up a bear. If you're attacked by a black bear, fight back—it'll likely flee. If it's a grizzly, play dead and hope you didn't have salmon for lunch.

After letting the afternoon heat steam off, by about 5:00 in the afternoon, you can get in some more miles before nightfall. It's best to start riding again about an hour before sunset and go as far as you can then. Also, the 1-hour-before-sunset rule of thumb allows you to more precisely plan where you'll end the day's riding.

If you'll be camping somewhere hot, avoid pitching your tent in the open desert. Ignore this advice at your peril: Along with being a beacon for all kinds of pests, you're in for a hotter, less comfortable night's sleep. At least set up next to a stand of bushes or scrub. You should also plan your days to end at higher altitudes on a mountain or mesa, which will decrease the temperature and increase your comfort level during the night.

Because water and food are critical and could be hard to come by in hotter climes such as deserts, you should pack to allow more room for

A hydration pack is an easy way to carry water, especially on an off-road ride. Double your water supply by slipping in a second bladder.

supplies. Figure that you need 1 pint of water for every 10 miles. Designate one of your bottles as your energy-drink bottle. As you're going along during the ride, alternate sips of water and energy drink every 5 to 10 minutes to replace the electrolytes you're sweating out.

So how do you carry enough water for 100-mile days? Along with adding as many water bottle mounts as your frame can stand (hopefully, at least three), you can strap on a hydration system that's like a minibackpack with a bladder for water. Look for one that has at least a 100-ounce bladder. A trick to easily double your fluid-carrying capacity is to buy a spare bladder, fill it, and tuck it in the backpack along with the other. Most hydration packs easily expand to accommodate tools and other supplies, so another bladder of water will easily slip in. Another option: Pack along water in small, pint-size water bottle containers. This way, you can balance your load and avoiding carrying all your water in one cumbersome container.

You need water on the inside and the outside. When the temp turns up, especially close to triple digits, squirt some water over your head every 30 minutes or so. It'll cool you off and keep your body temperature lower.

It's also a good idea to wear a jersey with a mesh front to allow air to flow through. (Women should wear a sports bra underneath, of course.) And be vigilant about applying sunscreen to all parts of your exposed body. Use a waterproof SPF 45 so it'll be around when your sweat starts pumping. Apply some as you're getting your bike ready for the day's ride, then again right before you hop on. You should use a lot more sunscreen than you think—an ounce per exposed area. An ounce is enough to cover your index and middle fingers—squeeze some on there and then apply that amount to any of the following areas that aren't covered by clothing:

- Head, face, and neck
- Left arm
- Right arm

- Upper back
- Lower back
- Upper front torso
- Lower front torso
- Left upper leg
- Right upper leg
- Left lower leg
- Right lower leg

Don't forget your lips, your ears, and the backs of your hands. Reapply sunscreen after about 4 hours on the bike, or sooner if you sweat like Niagara Falls.

To avoid getting the shapes of your helmet vents burned onto your scalp, wear a neckerchief or cycling cap under your helmet. This'll also help keep the sweat out of your eyes.

BUNDLE UP IN THE COLD

Plunging into bitter cold is something you'll rarely do without preparation. But whether you're planning a long haul through Jack Frost's backyard or you just want to be prepared for a cold spell over a mountain pass, this information will help.

First, if you know you'll be riding through the cold, allow yourself more time. For longer tours, plan for 1 or 2 days off the bike per week. This'll allow your body to recoup and add a cushion of time in case you run into really severe weather. You should also plan on allowing more time each day for getting dressed, packing, and postride maintenance and cleaning. If you're going to be camping, this means stopping maybe 2 hours earlier than you would normally, to allow plenty of time to set up camp before dark.

COLD-TEMP WARNING

A brisk breeze can be invigorating as you're going through the chilly countryside nowhere near traffic. But there's a difference between that slight cold sensation and hypothermia. Here are the warning signs of hypothermia's progression.

Mild. You're shaking and your hands and feet turn white. Your pulse may temporarily quicken, and your dexterity slows noticeably. Body temperature is about 95°F.

Moderate. Shivering slows—as does your heart rate—while your muscles stiffen. Temperature is about 91°F.

Severe. Your body parts turn blue and you're unable to move. Your body temp drops to 86°F or below.

Put as much planning into your wintry wardrobe as into planning your route. The word you need to know: layering. Instead of wearing one bulky piece of warm clothing, such as an overcoat, build your cold protection layer by layer. Several thinner layers of clothing are more versatile, since you can peel them off or put them on as the weather changes. The most important thing: Keep cold air off your chest and torso. If it's cooler than 60°F, it's time for a long-sleeved jersey and a vest or light jacket. It's also easier to pull stuff off than to not have it on and end up scrounging for trash bags to use as an emergency windbreaker/ insulator. Here's how you can build three layers of protection and which kinds of fabrics are good for each.

1. Base Layer

The clothes: Undershirt, shorts, balaclava, headband, helmet liner, glove liner, socks

The fabrics: Look for lightweight, snug-fitting fabrics that wick moisture from the skin so you won't feel the sweat. Avoid anything cotton on this layer. Instead, go for polypropylene, Thermastat, Field-sensor, CoolMax, Capilene, Dri-FIT, or Thermax.

2. Insulating Layer

The clothes: Jersey, vest, arm and leg warmers, tights

The fabrics: This layer will trap warmth and continue to transport moisture away from your body. Some items incorporate windproof barriers. Look for fabrics such as Polartec, Therma-FIT, wool, Wind-Stopper, Gore XCR, and Therma Fleece.

3. Outer Layer

The clothes: Jacket, rain suit, vest, helmet cover, insulated gloves, oversocks, booties

The fabrics: These range from lightweight (for fending off rain and wind) to coated, thicker fabrics for lots of protection. Waterproof jackets should have armpit zippers, side vents, or flap vents to reduce internal heat buildup. Cuff closures should be snug. Look for fabrics such as Silmond, Climaguard, nylon, Scotchgard, Gore-Tex, or Activent.

Once you're suited up for the chilly stuff, you should also get your bike ready. Cold-weather bike equipment is similar to the kind you'd use for rainy rides: fenders, mud flaps, perhaps mudguards, and possibly a lighting system for the bike because it's usually darker earlier in snowy climes. Choose a light with easy-to-replace batteries, such as AA.

HANDLE HIGH ALTITUDE

The higher you ride, the more beautiful the vistas—and the more adjustments your body has to make to the altitude. You may feel the effects of altitude as low as 4,000 feet, but most people notice a difference by the time they're 6,000 feet up. The thin air makes you feel out of breath easier and quicker, and its lower oxygen level makes your heart work harder to deliver oxygen to your muscles. You body adjusts by producing more oxygen-carrying red blood cells. But it can take a week before you adjust to altitude and feel normal.

You're getting altitude sickness if you have a pounding headache, lethargy, loss of appetite, and shortness of breath. The best remedy: Go down the mountain and recuperate.

Dehydration risk is also higher at higher altitudes because your body purges fluid as it acclimates. So make sure to drink more—shoot for 3 to 4 quarts a day. Avoid alcohol, smoking, and caffeine, since all of these sap vital body fluids. And don't pound up climbs, especially early in a tour with higher elevations. Take it easy and enjoy the views. You should also add more carbs to your diet, so that they make up about 70 percent of your total calorie intake.

CHAPTER 10

Maintenance
and Out-There
Repairs

How to prep your bike for your big trip—plus the 10 most common emergency fixes

There are two types of people in the world. One type consists of those who regale in the subtly complex beauty of the inner workings of the bicycle, who marvel at the fact that physicists can't easily explain why a bike stays upright, who admire the precision of carbon-fiber components working in harmony, and who spin hex wrenches, constantly tinkering with their two-wheeled mechanical wonders. Then there are people who don't like to get their hands dirty.

This chapter is for both of those types. On a tour, you rely on your bike more than at any other time. Your bike transports you from point A to point Z, but if you neglect maintenance or fail to learn the most basic of repairs—the flat fix—you're likely to get stuck at point L, a boring place nowhere near point A or Z that will become incredibly more awful when it starts raining. Even if you're planning to ride a fully supported tour on a rental bike, you can use this tried-and-tested maintenance wisdom to keep you rolling instead of waiting for the sag wagon.

These handy tips won't make you a master mechanic, but you'll be able to properly prep your bike before a trip and make the most vital in-the-field repairs. If bike touring is about discovering the world and yourself, maintenance and repair is one of those discoveries. With this know-how, you can experience the feeling of bringing a bike back to life—just as on a good, long ride, you'll attain a sense of can-do that can't be undone when you return to your 9-to-5.

And if you'd still rather be spooning sorbet with clean fingers, that's okay, too. This chapter also tells you how to have a shop prep your bike before a tour. You'll be a smarter consumer and better prepared for your trip. Clean hands or not, you'll look forward to what's over the next hill instead of dreading what'll go wrong next.

PRETRIP MAINTENANCE CHECKLIST

You wouldn't fly off without marking off a packing checklist, and you shouldn't leave home on a tour without running through a bike main-tenance checklist. This ounce of prevention is worth miles and miles of pounding the pavement and may save your vacation. Even if you don't do these pretrip checks yourself, it's important you know what they are so you'll know what to ask a shop to do. Leave plenty of time—at least 2 weeks—before your trip to do these checks, so you have time to fix anything that's wrong.

☐ **1. Check bolt tightness.** This doesn't mean you have to tighten every bolt on your bike. Instead, you should do just as we said: *Check* the tightness. Use a hex wrench to make sure the bolts are secure. Don't turn them so tight that they creak, or you'll strip or snap something. For a complete bike bolt checkup, start at the front and work your way to the rear. Be sure to include the handlebar stem bolts, stem steerer bolts, brake mounting bolts, brake pad bolts, seatpost bolt, and crankarm bolts. These are more likely to work loose and cause you to become a major contributor to your orthodontist's Porsche fund. If you've noticed bolts that keep loosening, particularly the rack bolts, add some Loctite to the threads.

Loctite secures bolts that could wiggle loose over long rides.

☐ **2. Check tire wear and tubes.** A tire is fresh if all the knobs have tall, square edges. There's slight wear when the center knobs are worn and peripheral treads are jagged. Your tires should be replaced if any knobs come loose or when casing shows slices or cuts. Front tires tend to last about twice as long as rear.

You'll also need to replace any tube with a slow leak. While it's not a big deal to reinflate a tire before rides at home, on a tour a leaky tube

could leave you stuck out in the middle of nowhere. To replace it, unhook your brakes and undo any quick-release (QR) to remove the wheel. Deflate the wheel and use a tire lever to pry the tire from the rim. Two or

Replace tires if the knobs start to show signs of wear like this.

three levers may make this easier: Use one to pry while using the others to hold the section of tire you've already opened. Pull the tire and tube off the rim. Before you put in the new tube, rub a light coat of baby powder over it and slightly inflate it to about 10 psi. This will make it easier to install and may help prevent the tube from sticking to the tire and potentially causing tears and flats. Position the new tire so that the label is over the valve stem hole. In addition to following cycling's traditional style, this makes it easier to spot the valve when you need to pump up your tire. To slip the tire back on the rim, reverse the process of taking it off, using tire levers, if needed, to slide it back into place. For the last section, use the palms of your hands to roll the bead into place. Reinflate the tire, then spin it while looking at where the tire and rim meet. If the bead wobbles, it's not properly seated. Deflate the tire, pinch it in the area where the wobble occurred, reinflate, and check again. Reinstall the wheel and reattach the brakes.

☐ **3. Scrub it down.** A clean bike is a happy bike. And a happy bike makes for a happy tour. You don't need to polish every nook and cranny, but at the very least, clean the drivetrain. Dirt trapped in your drivetrain will become a noisy shifting nightmare. With a mixture of degreaser, soap, and water, use a sponge to clean the rings and cogs. To avoid getting water in your rear hub, remove the back wheel and angle it at 45 degrees to allow water to wash off.

Apply degreaser along the length of the chain as you turn the crank backward. Use an old toothbrush or nylon bristle brush to loosen the grime, giving the cassette and chainrings a good scrubbing as well.

☐ **4. Clean the cables or replace frayed ones.** To create slack in the derailleur cables, shift into the largest cog in the rear, then upshift back into high gear without turning the cranks. This allows you to remove the housing from the frame stops. To make brake cables slack enough to remove them from the stops to clean them, either unhook the brakes or flip the QR levers, depending on your brake type. Wipe the exposed cable with a rag to remove old lubricant and debris. With a

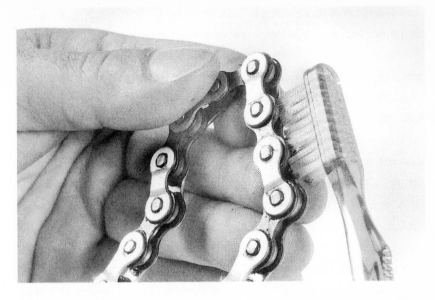

An old toothbrush is one of the best ways to scrub grime out of a chain.

Cleaning and lubing cables near the cable stops will improve shifting.

small blob of medium-weight bike grease on your fingertip or a few drops of lube, smear a light coat along the length of the cable. Work the grease back and forth over the cable, leaving just a thin coat. Replace the housing. Repeat for the front derailleur.

As for a frayed cable, if the damage is at the end, after the anchor bolt, there's not too much to worry about; the cable is still strong. To polish up the look of your bike, though, you can use cable cutters to trim the unsightly fray and then add a cable cap. However, if there is fraying along the length of the cable, this means the cable could possibly break or, at the very least, make for sloppy shifting or poor braking. You'll need to replace any cable that's frayed in the middle. First loosen the anchor bolt on the brake caliper or derailleur with a hex or box wrench. Remove the cable from the housing; you may need to cut a bad fray first to slide it through. Push the new cable back through the lever and housing and reattach to the anchor bolt.

☐ **5. Check chain wear.** Click into the largest chainring and the smallest cog. Then, with an inch ruler, measure the chain at the section

Match up ruler hash marks with the chain-pin centers. If the pin at the 12-inch mark isn't aligned in the center, get a new chain.

that stretches from the lower pulley to the bottom of the chainring. Align the 0 mark of the ruler in the center of one pin. The hash mark at 12 inches should match up with the center of the pin there. If the mark is closer to the edge of the pin or not aligned with the pin at all, the chain has stretched, and it's time to replace it.

There are also tools that more accurately measure wear. And if you've kept track of mileage, you might note that it's usually time to replace your chain after 1,500 to 2,000 miles. For lots of people, that's once or twice a year. Your chain might have special links that allow you to remove it by unclipping the side plates. If not, you'll need a chain tool specific to your type of chain. Use the chain tool to spin a pin until it pops out of the chain. Then size the new chain to the old one, removing links, if needed. Use the chain tool again to push the pin back into place. You'll probably have to flex the chain laterally to loosen the new pin and allow the chain to move without binding.

☐ **6. Lube the chain.** With the chain in the middle chainring and the middle of the cassette, lube about five sections of the chain. This will put oil onto the chain and the cog's teeth where they meet and

Drip lube on the rollers and wipe off any excess.

WHAT'S THE RIGHT LUBE
FOR YOUR TOUR?

If you'll be riding in wet conditions, look for a wet lube. If you're going somewhere where there's lots of dust, opt for a dry lube.

nowhere else, limiting the buildup on the gears and pulleys. Rotate the cranks and use a drip bottle to apply lube directly on the silver rollers in the center of the chain. Wipe off excess oil with a clean cloth. Or, if you prefer to use an aerosol lubricant, hold a rag behind the chain and send a stream of lube onto the chain. Rotate the cranks backward to expose another dry section of the chain, and repeat the process until the entire chain is lubed. Before you put down the rag, take an extra minute to clean any gunk off the derailleur, pulleys, and chainrings.

☐ **7. Examine the brake pads.** You may be able to extend the life of worn pads by using sandpaper to sand them flat. But if the pads are so

Removing debris from brake pad channels will improve braking power.

run-down that they're no longer grooved, it's time to replace them. With either a hex or box wrench, remove the old brake pads, noting the placement of the spacers on either side of the brake caliper. You'll want to reinstall the new brake pads with the same configuration. When you put the new pads into place, align them so they're not touching the tire or hanging below the rim. You want them to be centered on the rim. A trick to make this easier is to have a friend gently hold the brakes as you move the pad around. Then, as you tighten the bolt to secure the pads, slip a business card or other thin piece of cardboard under the rear third of the brake pad as the brake lever is applied and you're tightening the pad bolt. This will slightly toe the brake pad forward, which will reduce squealing.

☐ **8. Replace old handlebar tape.** If the tape is worn, dirty, and less comfortable to grip, remove it by cutting off any that's secured near the center of the bar and then unwinding. You'll need to gently push up the brake lever hoods to remove the old tape. Begin wrapping new tape tightly around the underside end of the bar so that about half the width

For a cushier grip on the top of the bar, wind bar tape in closer segments.

of the tape puckers over the end. You'll use this extra lip to push into the bar before finishing with the end cap. Wrap the tape toward the bike, overlapping one-third to half of the width of the tape. If you're working on the right-side bar, wrap counterclockwise; on the left bar, wrap clockwise. When you get to the lever, wrap the tape around it in a figure eight to prevent any bar from showing. This'll earn you style points. As you finish on the top of the bar and come to the end of the tape, use scissors to slice off a triangle-shaped wedge so the tape will lay flat in the final inch or so.

☐ **9. Check your tools.** That bunch of rusty relics bundled up in an old sock in your seatpack won't cut it where you're going. Plus, it may not have everything you need when help is hours away. As a bare minimum traveling tool kit, you should have:

- A minitool that includes a spoke tool, a chain-breaking tool, and all the sizes of hexes and screwdrivers to match the bolts on your bike.

- A pump.

A minitool should include a chainbreaker and all hex tools that match your bike's bolts.

FIVE THINGS
YOU SHOULDN'T REPLACE
BEFORE YOUR TOUR

1. Your whole bike—not even with an identical setup. Ride any new bike for at least 2 weeks before a tour. Even if you were to buy a new bike exactly like your current one, the setup could be slightly different, possibly causing you an uncomfortable ride. Plus, you wouldn't have time to perform any tweaks a new bike might need, such as trueing spokes or tightening steering.

2. Saddle. Your butt most likely has gotten used to your current saddle. And that trusty old seat has even changed its contours to fit your specific tush. A new saddle would need maybe a month to feel as comfortable and could give you saddle sores—and you don't want the break-in period to coincide with a tour.

3. Handlebar or stem, especially not with one that's a different size. While moving a handlebar a centimeter up, down, forward, or back may sound like a minor change, it can have a major impact on your comfort level. So swapping out a bar or stem could cause you to fatigue faster and suffer muscle aches.

4. Any major component, such as a new fork. Such components often require a little field testing to adequately tweak them. For instance, just hopping on a new fork without riding it beforehand may make for a harsher ride than you expect. Also, a tour is not the time to discover any defects.

5. Pedal system. You shouldn't be learning how to click in and out of a new pedal on a tour. You need your concentration for those amazing vistas and roads you've never ridden before. You'll likely have one silly, slow-motion fall because of a new pedal system. That's bad travel mojo.

OR JUST TAKE IT TO THE SHOP

If you're not up for prepping your bike yourself, take it to the shop at least 2 weeks before your trip. That'll allow lots of time to get the bike back for a few days of final shakedown riding and last-minute adjustments before you leave. Tell the mechanic you're leaving for a tour and ask him to specifically check everything in the pretour checklist. In addition, ask the mechanic to check the wheels for true and correct tension. For this kind of tune-up, expect to pay between $60 and $120. And don't forget to bring back a souvenir for the mechanic.

- A tire boot that'll temporarily patch a hole in a tire. This is a tough piece of rubber; some types have adhesive sides to stick in place.

- A fresh patch kit. If you haven't replaced your patch kit since Madonna's last makeover, time for a new one. Glue dries up, sometimes even in unopened containers.

- Three tire levers, to remove even the tightest tire.

- Small (about an ounce) bottle of lube. This'll quiet squeaks and help keep your chain running smoothly.

☐ **10. Replace worn cleats.** To make this lots easier, first use a pen to trace the outline of the old cleat on the sole of your shoe. This will allow you to reposition the new cleat without much trial and error. Using a hex wrench or screwdriver, remove the old cleat. You may first need to clean the bolt head using some solvent or degreaser. Before putting on the new cleat, be sure to apply grease to the threads on the bolts. This will prevent these bolts from seizing. Cinch down the bolts with the new cleat in place, following the outline on the sole of the shoe.

THE 10 MOST COMMON OUT-THERE REPAIRS

Unfortunately, no matter how thorough the pretour tune-up, bad things sometimes happen to good riders. Here are the most common emergency fixes that tour guides and *Bicycling* magazine's readers, writers, and editors have come across in their travels all over the world. With these easy, step-by-step remedies, you'll be able to save the day for yourself or your riding buddies. For a flat-tire-repair cheat sheet that you can remove from the book and fold into your seatpack, see page 221.

Flat Tire

Ever since Ignaz Schwinn threw a pair of pneumatic tires onto his newfangled safety bicycle in 1933, cyclists have waged an ongoing battle with the world's most common bike breakdown: the flat tire. Whether you run over nails in Nairobi or thorns outside of Tulsa, a flat will stop you cold. If you're stubborn or oblivious, you can ride for miles on your rims—provided you stay on smooth pavement. But it takes only one small pothole or stone to total the rims. Plus, the tire will be toast within about 100 feet.

Even on a fully supported tour, help may be hours away, so learning this repair will get you back on the road in a few minutes. It's easy and the dirt is minimal—honest. Just follow these five steps.

1. If it's your rear wheel that flatted, click into the smallest cog. Shift into the hardest gear and turn the pedals so that the chain moves into the smallest cog. This makes it easier to remove and replace the wheel, because the chain is more out of the way.

2. Remove the wheel. Flip the QR and spin it five or six times to loosen it. Unhook the brake cable or flip the cable release to move the pads away from the rim. To remove the front tire, push it straight down. For the rear wheel, you'll need to push forward and down, being sure to angle the wheel to the left to allow the chain to come off the cogs.

3. Remove the tire and tube. With your thumb and forefinger, pinch the tire bead all the way around the wheel. Put the wheel on the ground between your feet. Grab the tire and press down, then pull it up, over to the side, and off the rim.

If your tire is harder to remove, the following three tips will help. (Of course, the best way to avoid struggling with tight tires is to make sure *before* your trip that you can easily remove and replace them.)

• Use tire levers. Slip the spooned tip of one tire lever between the tire and rim. Pry the second lever into the space between the first lever and the rim and tire. Lift the second lever to further pry the tire from the rim. Then push along the rim, moving the tire up and off.

To remove a tight tire, slip one lever under the bead while pushing along the rim with another.

HOW TO PATCH A TUBE

Maybe you're cheap or maybe you're traveling in some part of the world where bike tubes are a black-market luxury. Patching is the answer.

Locate the hole in the tube by pumping air into it and listening or feeling for where the air comes out. Mark the hole or even enlarge it so it's easy to see. Lay the tube flat with the hole facing up. Wipe the tube clean and rough up the area around the hole with the sandpaper or buffer included in a patch kit. Don't skip this step; the tube has compounds on its surface that can prevent the patch from sticking. Rough up about a 1½-inch circle around the hole.

Coat the rough area with a thin layer of cement. Follow the directions on the glue tube, which may require that you allow the glue to air-dry and become tacky for a few minutes before putting on the patch. The patch should be large enough to cover the puncture by at least ½ inch on all sides. Don't touch the adhesive side of the patch as you apply it. Hold the patch firmly centered over the hole and allow it to set. Follow the directions on the tube for how long to allow the glue to set.

Before putting the tube back into the tire, inflate the tube and listen or feel for air coming out around the patch.

This technique works for most tires, but if a tire has a really tight bead, you may need to use three levers. Wedge the first between the tire and rim. Hook the other end into the spokes. Wiggle another tire lever into the space the first one made. Scoot it as far down the rim as you can, then hook the end of the second tire lever into the spokes. Use the third lever to pry the tire from there.

• Soap it down. If you have any soap handy or can slip into a bathroom and borrow a handful, coat the bead with the slippery stuff.

This'll allow the bead to slip over the rim more easily and let the tire levers move into place. No soap? You can just use water from a bottle or hydration pack as a lube.

• Pinch and pull. Stretch the tire bead by pinching the sides together and pulling every section all around the rim. This move is similar to the one you use to take off a tire by hand, but you go all the way around the wheel pinching and pulling up the tire.

4. Find the damage. Run your hand around the inside of the tire to feel for glass or thorns, and visually examine the sidewalls of the tire and rim. Make sure the flat-causer isn't still lodged in the tire before you install a new tube. If there's nothing poking through the tire, find the hole in the tube by inflating it and listening for the air. If there are two pinch marks, you have a pinch flat that may have been caused by too-low pressure or from hitting an obstacle such as pothole. Be sure to add more air next time.

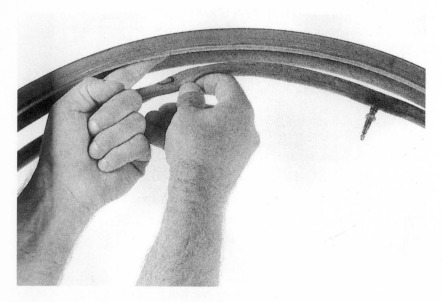

Run your finger along the inside of the tire to check for sharp objects.

NO SPARE, NO PATCHES, NO PROBLEM

Even with no spare tube or patches, and with civilization (and the sag wagon) miles away, a flat doesn't mean you're camping for the night.

After removing the wheel and tire, cut the tube at the site of the leak, then knot the ends together as tightly as possible. Wrestle the tube back into the tire and onto the rim; it'll fit more tightly than before. Once the tire is back on, inflate to minimal pressure: 25 to 30 psi for mountain tires and 60 to 70 for road. This isn't a leakproof or long-term fix, and you'll probably have to reinflate about every 20 minutes.

Another crude but effective way to keep rolling without a tube or patches: Pack leaves into the tire until it's as solid as possible. This'll probably wreck your tire, but you'll be able to ride until you get help.

Cutting and knotting a tube will get you to the next stop.

While the tire and tube are off the rim, inspect the spokes to be sure none are poking through the rim tape, puncturing the tube. Usually you can tell by running your hand along the tape or looking for holes in the tape.

5. Put it back. Slip one sidewall of the tire back on the rim. For a tight tire, use the palms of your hands to push up and roll the tire in place. Put a tube in the tire, slide the other sidewall into place, and inflate the tire. When it's about halfway inflated, spin the wheel to ensure that the bead is seated. If the bead is not on the rim properly, there will be a bulge in the tire where it meets the rim. To fix, deflate, tuck in the bulge, and reinflate. Often, the bead doesn't seat properly because the tube gets snagged between the tire and rim. Deflate and pinch together the tire's sidewalls while wiggling.

Use your thumbs and then palms to roll the last section of tire bead in place.

Once it's inflated, slip the wheel into the dropouts and press the frame down on it to ensure that it's in the frame correctly. Tighten the QR. Reattach the brakes. Before riding off, spin the wheel to be certain that it's still properly centered between the brakes and that the pads don't touch the tire.

Hole in Tire

While doing your postflat postmortem to find the cause, you may discover that the likely culprit is a sharp pointy thing in your tire. In addition to patching or replacing the tube, you'll need to cover the hole in the tire, or else the tube will bulge out and cause another flat within a few yards.

Remove the tire from the rim. On a longer tour, you may be packing a spare tire, so it's just a matter of swapping one for another. Otherwise, you'll have to cover the hole. Some tool kits come with self-adhesive tire boots, but you can also use an energy-bar wrapper or a folded-up dollar bill. If you have a patch kit, dab a little bit of glue around the hole to keep the patch in place. Some people have even used bubble gum in a pinch. Press the boot firmly in place and check it again as you finish putting the tube and tire back on the rim.

When you reinflate the tube, keep an eye on the hole to be sure the tube doesn't start to bulge through. If it does, deflate the tube, remove the tire, and find a sturdier tire patch.

A word of caution: This fix works well for holes an inch or smaller. A larger hole will tend to allow the tube to eventually bulge out, so keep an eye on it as you ride. No matter what size the hole is, replace the tire as soon as you're able.

Rubbing Brakes

Unless you're into resistance training on a tour, it's bad for your brakes to rub your rims all the time. Especially if you've just transported or unpacked your bike, check to be sure the wheels are seated in the drops. Loosen the QR lever, press down firmly on the seat, then retighten the

QR. If the brakes rub the rim only on certain spots when the wheel turns, then you need to true the wheel (check out "Wobbly Wheel" on page 176). But if a pad rubs constantly, you have brake troubles.

The temporary fix is to dial in the barrel adjuster near the brake

Shimano brake centering screw

Campagnolo brake centering screw

lever. Turning it clockwise will loosen the cable, moving the brake pads farther from the rim. However, this may mean the brakes will lose stopping power and you'll have to pull back farther on the levers to engage the brakes. Another temporary fix is to flip the brake release. (On a

Mountain bike centering screw

Adjustment knob on disc brake

Campagnolo brake, this is the button on the lever; on Shimano, the brake release is near the brake calipers.) This may solve the rubbing but leave you without the use of the brake.

If the brake still rubs, dial the centering mechanism on the brake calipers. Some brakes have these screws on both sides of the brake arms, others have them on one side only. You'll need a small hex tool or screwdriver. Turning the screw clockwise will increase the spring tension and move the pad away from the rim. Turning the screw counterclockwise moves the pad the other way.

Lost Bolt

Especially on longer trips, bolts will simply work themselves loose. With the wind rushing through your helmet, you may not even notice that a derailleur cable bolt has dropped off and headed north while you've kept rolling south. Finding a replacement bolt can be a matter of convenience, to fix a rattling water bottle cage, or of necessity, to reattach that derailleur or brake cable so you can shift or stop.

However, you don't need to ride with a pocket full of replacement bolts. Depending on your components, the bolts on your bike are often interchangeable. For example, water bottle bolts often work as replacements for brake hardware such as derailleur clamp bolts or cable anchor bolts along with cleat mounting bolts. Another handy example: The bolt on the top of most threadless headsets is an exact fit for many clamp-on-style seat binders.

Noisy Drivetrain

A constant, annoying clickety-clack from your drivetrain means that your gears aren't adjusted properly. You hear that noise if your rear derailleur cable is too tight or too loose. Most often, the problem is that the cable is loose. First figure out whether the sound is coming from the front or rear derailleur. Then dial that derailleur's adjuster knob (often located where the cable leads into the shifters or along the down tube) one-quarter turn counterclockwise (looking at it from the rear of the bike). If that turn makes it better but you've still got a slight click, go another quarter turn. If counterclockwise didn't help, dial the adjuster back to the original position and turn it a quarter turn clockwise. Usually a quarter to a half turn will have you running smoothly again.

Snapped Cable

When a cable breaks, it usually does so at the anchor bolt, where it's crimped and stressed. To fix a broken brake cable, you can usually free enough cable to clamp back to the anchor bolt by dialing in the barrel adjusters at the brake lever or on the brake body. You effectively shorten the housing, which is the same as lengthening the cable. If you need more brake cable, remove the spacers between your brake pads and brake arms. You might not be able to precisely angle the pads for

Wedge a small stick through the derailleur as an emergency fix for a snapped cable.

brake toe-in and alignment, but it'll give you enough extra cable to reach the anchor bolt.

Choose brakes over shifting: If there's no way the brake cable will reach or if it broke somewhere other than at the anchor bolt, either install a spare one or swap in a derailleur cable. (Install it according to the instructions on replacing frayed cable on page 154.) Because a shifter cable has smaller ends and won't fit in the brake lever slots properly, you'll have to tie the end around the cable holder.

Two other options for fixing a front derailleur if you don't want to ride in the small ring and don't have spare cable: Pull the remaining cable taut and secure it underneath a water bottle cage bolt; or shoehorn a pebble or twig between the front derailleur and the seat tube to prop the derailleur into a larger gear for the rest of the ride.

Broken Chain

Along with a flat tire, a broken chain is a common, yet entirely debilitating, snafu. A busted chain in the middle of nowhere can turn your

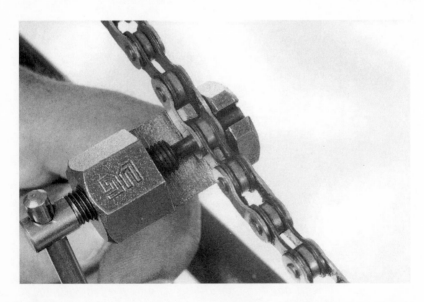

Slowly push the pin so there's a small lip protruding from one plate.

bike into an expensive, slow hobbyhorse. To fix it, you'll need a chain tool, part of most good minitools and an absolute must on your touring checklist. In addition to repairing a broken chain, you can use the following technique to remove links that have twisted and become hung up in the drivetrain.

To get more slack in the chain, thus making it easier to work with, click the drivetrain into the smallest cog and smallest ring. Thread the chain through the derailleurs and drop it around the bottom bracket. It's easiest to work with the section of chain that runs from the bottom of the lower pulley to the bottom of the rings. Position the chain tool on the inside of the bike so that you're pushing the pin to the outside. Slowly dial the pin out, but leave a small lip protruding from the plate. You may need to remove a link from the other end of the chain to match the open plates.

Wedge the inner link end of the chain into the outer link. The little bit of pin that protrudes should help hold the links together as you press

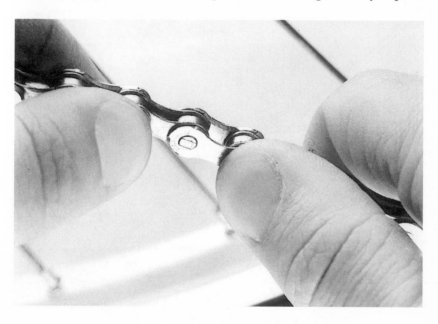

To prevent binding, flex the chain laterally with your thumbs.

the pin back with the chain tool. Use the chain tool to slowly press the pin back through the links until the pin protrudes equally from each side. Flex the joined link laterally by grabbing the chain on either side of the link with your thumbs and bending sideways, back and forth, a few times. This unkinks the chain so the newly installed pin doesn't bind the link where it's been installed.

Wobbly Wheel

When your wheel is out of true, you'll probably hear it before you see it wobbling. A rhythmic *shhh, shhh, shhh* from your brake pad is the telltale sound. Spin each wheel to figure out which has the wobble. Flip over the bike and use the brake pads as a guide. For really bad wobbles, you may need to dial in your brake cable barrel adjuster to move the pads away from the rim and allow the wheel to spin.

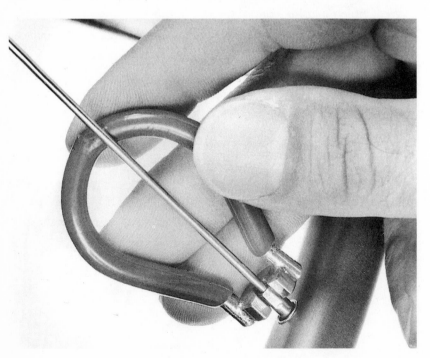

Tighten or loosen spoke nipples by quarter turns.

Find the two spoke pairs nearest to where the rim is close to or touching a brake pad. Spoke pairs are two spokes that lead to the same side of the hub. On the side where the rim touches the pad, use your minitool's spoke wrench to loosen the spoke nipples a quarter turn by turning counterclockwise as you're looking at the spoke through the rim. Then, tighten the other pair of spokes a quarter turn. When trueing a wheel, smaller turns are better. Repeat until the wobble is small enough that the wheel freely spins within the brake pads.

Before turning the bike upright and riding off, squeeze spoke pairs to check the tension of the spokes on the whole wheel. On the front wheel, the tension should be similar the whole way around. On the rear wheel, the drivetrain-side spokes are tighter than the nondrivetrain spokes. A spoke loose enough that you can wiggle it with two fingers means you have more trueing to do. After you squeeze the spokes, retest the true.

Check the spoke tension by squeezing spoke pairs.

Broken Spoke

The good news: A single broken spoke doesn't mean your wheel is instantly wrecked—you can keep riding on it as long as handling and braking are unaffected. The bad news: You can't keep riding with a broken spoke indefinitely, because eventually your wheel will go out of true and may collapse. To prevent a broken spoke from lashing your frame, thread it out through the hub or twist it around another spoke to keep it in place.

If you've brought an emergency replacement spoke, you can hook the curved end into the hub flange so that the head orientation is consistent with that of neighboring spokes. For example, if the heads alternate between facing out and in, be sure the replacement spoke head fits the pattern. Angle the spoke toward the rim, lacing it through the neighboring spokes in the same pattern as the rest of the wheel. Thread it into the spoke nipple and add tension. With the minitool spoke

Lash a single broken spoke around its neighbors.

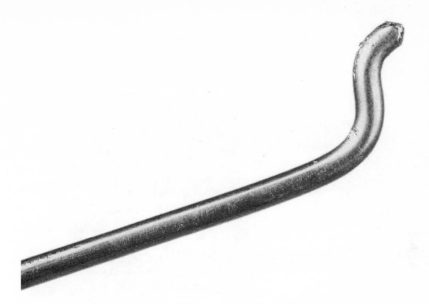

Hook the end of an emergency replacement spoke into the hub.

wrench, tighten it until it is at about the same tension as its neighbors, spinning the wheel to check for wobbles, and true as necessary.

Inspect the wheel to see if you can determine what caused the break: Maybe the rear derailleur jumped into the spoke, or the spoke may have broken under tension. A strange-but-true bike maintenance rule: Too-loose spokes are more likely to break than tight ones. This is because they're allowed to flex in ways they shouldn't, so they snap.

Mangled Rear Derailleur

To a cyclist, few sounds are so gut-wrenching or sights so de-pressing as a mangled rear derailleur. The tangled mess of chain, de-railleur, and maybe even spokes means you're going nowhere. But you can get rolling again, even if your derailleur is twisted beyond use.

First, look at the derailleur from the rear. If the derailleur hanger (the part of the frame where the derailleur is attached) is bent only a little,

Use the rear wheel as a lever to bend a mangled derailleur hanger.

with the pulleys just a few degrees from being parallel to the cogs, you can fix it by bending the derailleur back into place. Grab the derailleur around the upper part of the body, not the pulleys. Gently bend it back until the pulleys are aligned with the cogs. The most important word in that last sentence: *gently*. Let the pressure slowly build as you attempt the tweak, instead of making one heave-ho. Then, the best way to check the alignment is to look down at the pulley and cogs while standing over the bike.

If the derailleur is severely bent and pokes into the spokes in the lower gears, you need more leverage. (And you may have to replace spokes as well.) With a hex wrench, remove the derailleur bolt, then re-move the rear wheel and use the QR lever skewer to bolt the rear wheel onto the derailleur hanger. The rear wheel will now be mounted on your frame like a big steering wheel. Grab the wheel on opposite sides and use its leverage to straighten the hanger. Word of caution: Only bend steel frames like this. Steel can bend without losing much strength; however, aluminum and titanium hangers will often break before they bend.

Before you hop back on the bike, slowly spin the chain backward and look for twisted links. The pulleys will often jump or get caught on such links. Remove any twisted links using the techniques for fixing a broken chain on page 174. You may then have to avoid bigger cog and bigger chainring gear combinations because your chain will be shorter.

If the derailleur is twisted beyond use, you can limp to the next bike shop or rest stop by removing it completely and shortening the chain. You'll have to break the chain and make it shorter—long enough to fit around a gear you can stay in for the rest of the ride. Pedal lightly, because the chain won't be tensioned, so it might skip.

CHAPTER 11

Dream Trips

Your guide to the 10 best cycling destinations
on the planet

At certain places on the globe, terrain and culture collide to create environments so conducive to cycling that they're must-visits for anyone who pedals a bike. Go to any of these locales and you won't feel the least bit self-conscious about walking around off the bike in a helmet and bike shorts. At these destinations, cyclists are fully accepted—even catered to. These places are white stars of cycling: dense and intensely bright with the culture of the bike. The people who live there—and those who flock there—live to ride and ride to live.

Because these locales are steeped in cycling culture, they may even lead you to a greater appreciation of the sport. Best of all, these destinations are simply great places to take a vacation. Even traveling companions who might not be of the pedaling persuasion will have plenty to see and do, going for hikes, tasting wine and the local cuisine, or touring ruins.

These aren't the only great places to ride, but they're arguably the pinnacles. And the beautiful thing about cycling is that you can always find your own dream trip—and it may start in your own backyard.

In this chapter, we've made every effort to include up-to-date information to help you plan your dream trip. All this information was accurate at the time this book went to press. Remember, however, that tour companies change their offerings and routes from year to year. Prices can change even in midseason, which is why we don't mention them. Also, take the contact information with a grain of salt. Bike shops and tour companies open, close, and move. Web site URLs change, as do phone numbers. So you may have to use our suggestions as a starting point for your own research. Hey, at least we've given you a head start.

1. MOAB, UTAH

"Whether you pass through quickly or stay a lifetime, the spirit of the canyons will leave its mark on you. Sun-baked rock, twisted juniper, pothole puddles teeming with fairy shrimp and tadpoles—these images ring with the power of beauty, the power of the desert. Treasure them as wild things must be treasured."

—wilderness photographer Stephen Trimble

Mountain biking may have been born in California, but Moab has become the pinnacle destination for fat-tire riders. This area in eastern Utah is home to two of the most famous trails in the world: the Slickrock loop and the Porcupine Rim. The mind-bending terrain around this former mining town reveals how form meets function on a mountain bike, demanding the most out of both the bike and the rider. Because of the unbelievable traction on Slickrock, you can take yourself to the limits of speed and technical skills, swoop through fantastic moonscapes and Swiss-cheese rock formations, and fly out of deep bowls that were around long before BMXers eyeballed empty swimming pools.

And you don't need to go to an off-road extreme to immerse yourself in the area's natural splendor. Moab is nestled in a valley between sandstone cliffs and the Colorado River, which makes it a great starting point for road adventures. The south end of Moab is at the base of the

La Sal Mountains; 5 miles north is Arches National Park, with more than 2,000 natural stone arches; and 30 miles to the west is Canyonlands National Park.

Best Seasons

April through May and September through October

Tours

Dreamride: Small groups of no more than four client-riders on high-end bikes to remote areas around Moab; (435) 259-6419; www.dreamride.com

Moab Century Tour/Skinny Tire Festival: Scenic ride on LaSal Loop Road through Arches National Park and along the Colorado River, with 45-mile and 60-mile options; (435) 259-2698; www.skinnytirefestival.com

Nichols Expeditions: Half-day guided Slickrock rides to weeklong multisport tours throughout the White Rim area; (800) 648-8488; www.nicholsexpeditions.com

Rim Tours: Half-day and full-day excursions to Slickrock, Porcupine Rim, and other red-rock trails; (800) 626-7335; www.rimtours.com

Western Spirit Cycling: Fully supported camping trips with showers and guides doing the cooking in the evening; (800) 845-2453; www.westernspirit.com

Do It Yourself

Road Routes

Arches Ride: 41-mile out-and-back to Devils Garden

Needles Overlook Ride: 44-mile round-trip to the Needles Overlook and back

Mountain Rides

Hurrah Pass: An easy dirt road where you can take breaks to see petroglyphs and gaze at amazing canyon overlooks

Slickrock Trail: 12 miles of beautifully technical trail; ride the practice loop first

Contacts

Moab Information Center, (800) 635-6622, www.moab-utah.com, www.discovermoab.com

Utah Travel Council, (800) 200-1160, www.utah.com

Get There

Moab's Canyonlands Field Airport (CNY); or fly into Salt Lake City International (SLC) and drive about 240 miles southeast; or fly into Colorado's Walker Field Airport (KGJT) in Grand Junction and drive about 113 miles northwest

Bike Shops

Chile Pepper Bike Shop, 550½ North Main Street, Moab; (435) 259-4688, (888) 677-4688; www.chilebikes.com

Poison Spider Bicycles, 497 North Main Street, Moab; (800) 635-1792; www.poisonspiderbicycles.com

Slickrock Cyclery, 415 North Main Street, Moab; (800) 825-9791; www.moab-utah.com/slickrockcycles/

2. CALIFORNIA WINE COUNTRY

"The soil has sublimated under sun and stars to something finer, and the wine is bottled poetry. The smack of California earth shall linger on the palate of your grandson."

—writer Robert Louis Stevenson

Uncork a ride through these lush valleys and you'll taste the luxurious extremes of cycling. During a day of typically perfect weather, you ride a connect-the-dots route from winery to winery, sampling the best of the Sonoma and Napa Valleys, America's cradle of winemaking. Along quiet roads, daily mileage can easily vary from just 10 miles, with more time for sipping and sampling, to 100-mile days along the Russian River. On a mountain bike, the Californian extremes continue on the hundreds of miles of trails in the area. You can plunge down canyon trails, then bend your neck skyward as you look up to the giant redwoods.

Whether you hit the trails or the road, at night, the off-the-saddle attractions rival the magnificent riding. You'll please your palate with

world-class dining in indulgent settings overlooking the Pacific Ocean. After dinner, massage therapists are at your call, and in the morning, you can wake up to champagne breakfasts. Ah, extreme comfort.

Best Seasons

April through May and September through November

Tours

Andiamo Adventours: Romantic tours through Northern Napa and Southern Alexander Valleys; (800) 549-2363; www.andiamoadventours.com

Bicycle Adventures: One tour includes dinner at the Culinary Institute of America; (800) 443-6060; www.bicycleadventures.com

Getaway Adventures: Four-Valleys Ride—all northern California's wine country year-round tours; (800) 499-2453; www.getawayadventures.com

Napa Valley Bike Tours: Allows self-guided/guided flexibility, year-round tours; (800) 707-2453; www.napavalleybiketours.com

Trek Travel—Sonoma Valley and Napa Valley: Tour de France champ Greg LeMond goes along for some rides; (866) 464-8735; www.trektravel.com

Wine Country Bikes classic wine tour: Sample Napa and Sonoma, or go self-guided; (866) 922-4537; www.winecountrybikes.com

Do It Yourself

Road Routes

St. Helena–Yountville Loop: About 37 miles, much of it along the Silverado Trail; stop in Yountville for coffee and circle back to St. Helena

Sonoma–Congress Valley Loop: 35 miles with six wineries along the way; starts at Sonoma Valley Cyclery

Mountain Rides

Boothe-Napa State Park, St. Helena: Ride fire roads up to surround yourself with redwoods and visit historic buildings; (707) 942-4575

Boggs Mountain State Forest, Lake County: Singletrack weaves through this remote area (be sure to take loads of water), where the trails follow the contour of the land and don't constantly climb; (707) 928-4378

Contacts

The Napa Valley Conference & Visitors Bureau, (707) 226-7459, www.napavalley.com, www.winecountry.com

Get There

Napa County Airport (APC); or fly into San Francisco International (SFO) and drive about 50 miles north

Bike Shops

Bicycle Madness, 2500 Jefferson Street, Napa; (707) 253-2453;
www.bicyclemadness.com

Bicycle Works, 3335 Solano Avenue, Napa; (707) 253-7000

Sonoma Valley Cyclery, 20093 Broadway, Sonoma; (707) 935-3377;
www.sonomavalleycyclery.com

3. VERMONT IN AUTUMN

I make a great noise
Of rustling all day . . .

—from Robert Frost's "Gathering Leaves"

Roll into a Northeast autumn, and you ride into a crucible of change,
the place to wrap up your cycling for the season or to take your first
tour. A quilt of vivid red, brilliant yellow, and fading green leaves blankets the Vermont mountains, a place where you can make memories
that'll last much longer than the coming winter. Vermont rides take you
past farmland with traditional red barns, beside pristine lakes, through
covered bridges, and next to classic Colonial churches. You'll climb the
Adirondack and Green Mountains, and as leaves float down, descents
will become a colorful blur that'll make you feel like you're riding into
a Monet painting.

Trails in the northeast are a different kind of artwork, requiring an
artistry to master. Roots, rocks, and logs make the trail riding here
some of the most technical in the world. However, a rail-trail stretches
75 miles across the state for a smoother ride. Whichever route you take,
it'll feel like you're taking the less traveled road.

Best Season

September through October

Tours

Bike Riders Tours: Nice and easy tours that immerse you in the local culture; www.bikeriderstours.com

Bike Vermont: Guiding tours since 1976, they offer inn-to-inn lodgings and fine dining; (800) 257-2226; www.bikevermont.com

VBT: Specializes in smaller tours and has a variety to choose from; (800) 245-3868; www.vbt.com

Vermont Inn-to-Inn: Stay in country inns between riding either in Champlain Valley on road bikes or on Green Mountain on off-road bikes; (800) 838-3301; www.inntoinn.com

Do It Yourself

Road Routes

Notch Loop: 46 miles from Stowe to Jeffersonville and up the climb called Smuggler's Notch; www.bikestowe.com

Northeast Kingdom, near East Burke: The route takes you over rolling roads in the middle of 2,000 square miles of forest; www.eastburkesports.com

Mountain Rides

Cross Vermont rail-trail: 75 miles of gravel/ballast from Burlington to Wells River

Mount Snow: 45 miles of mountain biking singletrack, doubletrack, and ski trails, along with some of the most technical riding in the country (trails near base areas are good for learning); (800) 245-7669; www.mountsnow.com

Contact

Vermont Tourism Corporation, (800) 837-6668, www.travel-vermont.com

Get There

Fly into Burlington International Airport (KBTV) for northern trips; or fly into New York's Albany International Airport (ALB) and drive approximately 30 miles to get to more southern Vermont destinations

Bike Shops

Brattleboro Bike Shop, 165 Main Street, Brattleboro; (802) 254-8644; www.bratbike.com

The Mountain Sports and Bike Shop, 580 Mountain Road, Stowe; (802) 253-7919; www.bikestowe.com

True Wheels Bike Shop and The Basin Ski Shop, Killington; (802) 422-3234; www.truewheels.com

4. TOUR DE FRANCE

"Everything comes together for the Tour. The roads take on their own identity. There is a romance to them and they belong to the Tour. You couldn't have this race in any other country."

—three-time Tour champion Greg LeMond

Unabashedly and entirely justifiably, the Tour de France is the world's greatest race. Yet it is so much more than riders making their way around the country over 3 weeks in July. The Tour is a celebration, with a parade that blazes the route each day. It is the largest spectator event in the world, with an estimated 15 million fans watching along the route and a television audience of more than 250 million. The Tour is the high-tech testing ground for lust-inspiring cycling equipment. The Tour makes heroes, breaks dreams, and inspires awe. The Tour is life.

And as a cyclist, you can create your own intimate memories of the Tour. While NASCAR won't let fans take a few hot laps around Daytona, you can ride past the lavender fields at the base of Alpe d'Huez as you climb the fabled 21 switchbacks. You can also stop and take a picture among the sunflower fields. You can get a taste of the Tour with shorter trips where you ride an individual stage or follow the entire route, even finishing down the Champs Elysées to cheering crowds. *Vive le Tour!*

Tours

Backroads: Several packages ranging in length and varying degrees of ride difficulty; some trips start in Paris during the race's first week, others include the toughest climbs, such as Ventoux and Alpe d'Huez; (800) 462-2848; www.backroads.com

Breaking Away Tours: Tour RacePak trips combine race viewing with lots of riding; (310) 545-5118; www.breakingaway.com

Butterfield and Robinson: Luxury touring of the Tour course with high-end culinary experiences and posh lodgings; (800) 678-1147; www.butterfieldandrobinson.com

Graham Baxter Sporting Tours: Operates a fleet of buses transporting hundreds of cycling fans; has noncycling tourist weekend and longer tours that include riding every mountain stage; www.sportingtours.co.uk/index.html

Trek Travel: Known for behind-the-scenes access to teams; (866) 464-8735; www.trektravel.com

VeloSport Vacations: Trips may include access to racers along with insider guides; (800) 988-9833; www.velovacations.com

Do It Yourself

Ride along a stage route with 7,500 fans through the French *Velo* magazine–sponsored Etape du Tour; www.letapedutour.com

Or you can hook up with touring companies, such as CycloMundo Vacations (www.cyclomundo.com/vacations.htm) or Custom Getaways (www.customgetaways.com/tourdefrance.htm) to plan your own route while relying on some of their resources, such as maps and lodging guides

Another resource for following the Tour on your own is Lonely Planet's Cycling France (www.lonelyplanet.com), which includes a chapter on shadowing the race

5. DOLOMITES IN ITALY

"Imagine a place where hills roll endlessly, where warm sunshine is the rule, where a plate of pasta waits at the most remote summits. Think of a place where cyclists are so adored that when drivers shout out their car windows, they're offering encouragement and, maybe around the next bend, a sandwich."

—*Bicycling* magazine writer Dan Koeppel

In Italy, the coffee tastes better, the pasta sauce, zestier; breezes feel crisper—and bikes, more at home. There's a reason: It's because the coffee is better; sauce more zesty; breezes more crisp; and, of course, this is the country of bike legend, lore, and religion. Italy even has the Madonna del Ghisallo, the patron saint of cycling, and in a small

church north of Milan, you can get your bike blessed. But the true religious experience for cyclists is riding through the Dolomites, Italy's eastern Alps, just south of Innsbruck, Austria. Mountains rise in the distance like cathedrals. Rides dip back into valleys and follow long stretches of coast by castles and ancient Roman ruins. In some of the most scenic and sometimes challenging cycling in the world, curtains of rocks surround you as you ride up switchbacks to mountaintop medieval towns. You can chase your own Maglia Rosa, the pink leader's jersey of Italy's grand tour, the Giro d'Italia. You'll ride some of the most vertical landscapes in the world, climbing the stratified rock formations and rolling through famous passes such as Campolongo, Pordoi, Sella, and Gardena. You'll notice towns with the same name as bike parts, such as Selle. You'll also link small, quaint towns on narrow, quiet roads where, if you do encounter motorists, they'll be ones who expect and respect cyclists.

Best Season

Late June through July

Tours

Ciclismo Classico: Numerous themed vacations, from high-end cuisine to tough climbs; (800) 866-7314; www.ciclismoclassico.com

ExperiencePlus!: Also offers walking tours, and many guides are locals; (800) 685-4565; www.experienceplus.com

La Cima Tours: Weaves through quaint villages and connects some of the most beautiful and highest peaks in the country; (916) 641-2953; www.lacimatours.com

Do It Yourself

Holiday on 2 Wheels: Chain of hotels that tailor services to cyclists, including route planning and maintenance; www.italybikehotels.it

Lago di Garda: Home of the world's largest mountain bike festival, with 20,000 riders; about 3,000 miles of trails in the area

6. BRITISH COLUMBIA

"I think British Columbia very like heaven, or like what I should like my heaven to be, if ever I arrive so high—one mass of mountains, with mirrors of water mixed with them, torrents and forests, and roaring rhones."

—novelist M. P. Shiel

Welcome to the land of swooping switchbacks, the cutting edge of hard-core mountain biking, with routes forged more than a century ago, during the gold rush. Ride the singletrack here and you'll descend

through flower-filled alpine meadows. In British Columbia, you'll be in remote areas and be able to get away from it all. Or you can opt for ski resort cycling, such as Whistler Mountain. If you're looking for a challenge, there are technical singletrack, elevated trails, and 8-foot, hard-core jumps. Then, for the more laid-back BC experience, you can cruise along seaside road rides, where you connect loop after loop with ferry rides mixed in the middle.

Best Season

June through September

Tours

Fernie Fat-Tire Adventures: Singletrack tours around the small town of Fernie; (888) 423-7849; www.ferniefattire.com

Gravity Fed Adventures: Mountain biking trips along horse trails with cabins and tents; (250) 238-0170; www.gravityfedadventures.com

Great Explorations: Along with Kettle Valley tours, hosts Sea to Sky Trail Ride from D'Arcy to Squamish; (800) 242-1825; www.great-explorations.com

North Shore MTB Tours: Hard-core mountain bike riders only; stunt tours of some of the most difficult riding in the world; (847) 763-0011; www.cnscvb.com

Do It Yourself

Road Routes

3-Ferry Loop: About 50 miles beginning at Brentwood Bay and ferry to Mill Bay onto the Trans Canada Highway. Through rolling country-side, you'll ride through the town of Cowichan Bay. The next ferry will take you to Salt Spring Island, and after reaching Fulford Harbor, you'll ferry back to Schwartz Bay to roll back to the start.

Fraser Valley to Hope Loop: About 100 miles from the Pacific Ocean, along Fraser River and back along the Trans Canada Highway

Mountain Rides

Roller Coaster: A twisting singletrack built for speed among Pacific Spirit Park's 21 miles of trails

Whistler Mountain: 7,160 feet high; has about 60 miles of singletrack, along with 30 miles of trails around nearby Whistler Village

Contact

British Columbia Tourism Office, (800) 435-5622, www.hellowbc.com

Get There

Fly into Vancouver International Airport (YVR)

Bike Shops

Cove Bike Shop, 4310 Gallant Avenue, North Vancouver; (604) 929-1918; www.covebike.com

Cranky's Bike Shop, 25677 36th Avenue, Aldergrove; (604) 856-1688; www.crankysbikeshop.com

Simon's Bike Shop, 608 Robson Street, Vancouver; (866) 600-1181; www.simonsbikeshop.com

7. COLORADO ROCKIES

"I have hiked mountains throughout the West and seen many more around the globe in pictorial essays, and I think I am correct when I say that there is no place like Colorado. Our mountains are neither the oldest nor the youngest—in fact, they are about 65 million years old. What is remarkable is that they have weathered and crumbled to exactly the right degree to make them the most beautiful mountains in the world."

—wilderness photographer John Fielder

Colorado is America's altitude king. In its more than 50 mountain ranges, the state boasts three-fourths of the country's terrain above 10,000 feet. This means a journey to the Centennial State will fix just about any cycling jones you have: You can meander along from friendly town to friendly town with towering mountains as a backdrop. Or you can set a personal speed record screaming down one of the long, long descents. Tucked along the folds of the mountains are communities that are ingrained in cycling, such as Colorado Springs, home to the Olympic training facility and the perfect place to train America's best athletes. Of course, if you're a climber, these mountains are for you, with the highest paved road in the United States, the Trail Ridge Road in Rocky Mountain National Park. It climbs to an astounding and

breathtaking 12,183 feet. Eleven miles of the road are above the tree line, and bighorn sheep may race you up.

Mountain biking around the Rockies, especially around the Colorado Springs area, can vary from smooth fire roads to technical, rock-strewn singletrack. As you ride, you'll pop out of trees and have amazing overlooks before swooping down some of the longest single-track trails in the country.

Best Season

June through September

Tours

Ride the Rockies: A 6-day, almost 500-mile long, high-altitude tour averaging 60 to 65 miles and gaining 3,000 to 4,000 feet of elevation per day; www.ridetherockies.com

The World Outdoors: Based in Boulder, offers multisport trips along with catering to small groups and families; (800) 488-8483; www.theworldoutdoors.com

Pikes Peak Mountain Bike Tours: Allows you to pick the amount of climbing you want to do with shuttles to the tops and some rides that are about 95 percent downhill; (888) 593-3062; www.biketours.com

Do It Yourself

Road Routes

Trail Ridge Road: As you ascend the 48-mile road, you'll see the environment change from aspen forests and ponderosa pine to alpine tundra

Rabbit Ears Pass: Will take an hour to summit the 9,426-foot top that's 6 miles from Steamboat Springs, but only 15 minutes to get back

Mountain Rides

Pearl Pass: A famous ride that connects Aspen with Crested Butte

Boreas Pass: A rail-trail in Breckenridge that's about 22 miles of crushed stone and easy grades but with a beautiful backdrop

Contacts

Colorado Travel and Tourism Office, (303) 892-3885, www.colorado.com

Denver Metro Convention and Visitors Bureau, (800) 233-6837, www.denver.org

Get There

Fly into Denver International Airport (DEN) or the City of Colorado Springs Municipal Airport (COS)

Bike Shops

Colorado Cyclist, 3970 East Bijou Street, Colorado Springs; (800) 688-8600; www.coloradocyclist.com

Vecchio's Bicicletteria, 1833 Pearl Street, Boulder; (303) 440-3535; www.vecchios.com

Wheat Ridge Cyclery, 7085 West 38th Avenue, Wheat Ridge; (303) 424-3221; www.wheatridgecyclery.com

8. PACIFIC COAST HIGHWAY

"The face of the Earth as the Creator intended it to be."

—author resident Henry Miller

Stretching the length of America's western coast from Canada to Mexico for about 1,950 gorgeous miles is the Pacific Coast Highway.

Along the way, you'll experience a change in climates and surroundings. This ride is the ultimate change. Most people start north from the deep forests of the Pacific Northwest and shed rain gear as they spin south, saving the sunny climes as an end-of-the-ride reward. The solitude of the north contrasts with the busy California beachside roads you'll pass around Laguna. All along the way, you'll see beaches carved by God's special beach-cutting knife that leaves rugged, beautiful coastlines in it wake. Layers of clouds across the ocean burn off to your right as you cycle south. And to the left, layers of mountains fade into the lands. One of the most scenic portions of the ride begins at Point Lobos, a nature reserve south of Carmel, and continues along the coastline to the San Luis Obispo county line. Author Henry Miller lived in Big Sur, and this may be one of many places you'll linger along the way.

Best Season

May through October

Tours

For info on the Oregon Coast bike route, call the Bicycle Hotline, (503) 986-3556, or Oregon Coast Visitors Association, (888) 628-2101; www.visittheoregoncoast.com

Do It Yourself

Contacts

California Division of Tourism, (916) 322-2881, www.colorado.com

Oregon Tourism Commission, (800) 547-7842, www.traveloregon.com

Washington Tourism, (800) 544-1800, www.experiencewashington.com

Get There

Head to the top (northern) part by flying into Port Angeles, Washington, William R. Fairchild International Airport (CLM); or start at the bottom at San Diego International Airport (SAN)

9. ACROSS AMERICA

"In America, our origins matter less than our destination. This country was founded and built by people with great dreams and the courage to take great risks."

—former president Ronald Reagan

Dipping your wheel in the Pacific and, on the other side, in the Atlantic rewards you and your bike. Now the Adventure Cycling Association makes planning your cross-nation jaunt easier, with established routes across the north, south, and middle, along with accompanying maps. Whichever way you go, you're in for a haul. The shortest cross-country route is Imperial Beach, California, just south of San Diego,

to Jacksonville, Florida, at 2,328 miles. At 3,298 miles, San Diego to Madawaska, Maine, is second. Longest direct route across the United States is 3,681 miles, from Neahbay, Washington, to Key West, Florida.

For the fastest way to cross the country, hop in a paceline during the Race Across America (RAAM). The annual cross-country race has been called the Tour de France done the American way. Top individual racers pedal roughly 350 miles per day, burning 9,000+ calories and sleeping just 90 minutes. In addition to the near-insane soloists, teams of two, four, or eight riders race nonstop relays, covering more than 500 miles per day.

Tours

America by Bicycle: Ride coast to coast, including 29 tours from 5 to 29 days, with all motel lodging—no camping—and mechanical and sag support; (888) 797-7057; www.aabike.com

Crossroads Cycling Adventures: Long-distance fully supported tours, all motel lodging; ride 1 to 7 weeks; (800) 971-2453; www.crossroadcycling.com

The Big Race

Race Across America: You can't just hop in. You first have to put your body through an almost equally grueling qualifying race. For more information, see www.raceacrossamerica.org.

Do It Yourself

Transamerica Self-Contained Expeditions: Choose from several tested routes, and ride at your own pace; (800) 755-2453; www.adventurecycling.org

10. YOUR OWN BACKYARD

Almost all of this book has been devoted to pure how-to: the skills, tips, and tricks that enable you to select and enjoy cycling trips all over the world. There hasn't been much rhapsodizing about the pure fun of simply pedaling a bicycle. Here goes.

Your bike is discovery; your bike is freedom. It doesn't matter where

you are, when you're on your saddle, you're taken away. On a loop around your town, you'll feel that same motion and rush of wind as you did when you were on a trip through Asia. Close your eyes for an instant and you're back in Bangkok. That's the magic escape of a bicycle. It's like the best travel writing; it makes you feel like you're at the destination.

Even if you're not in a far-flung corner of the world, you can still feel like you're on an international adventure. Sure, it helps when one of your friends breaks into a corny Italian accent. But maybe you're also thinking about your last trip—how your Thursday night route climbs compare with those from your vacation or how you're looking forward to sipping some of that wine you brought back home. Along with sharing tales and reliving your trips, these familiar routes can be where you plan your next cycling getaway.

Finally, when you do take that dream trip, nothing beats coming home.

Resources

TOUR COMPANIES

Active Journeys
Variety of international destinations with biking and multisport tours
(800) 597-5594
www.activejourneys.com

America by Bicycle
Coast-to-coast tours
(888) 797-7057
www.abbike.com

Backroads
Variety of domestic and international destinations; biking, walking,
multisport
(800) 462-2848
www.backroads.com

Bicycle Adventures
A variety of domestic destinations along with Canada and New Zealand
(800) 443-6060
www.bicycleadventures.com

Bike Riders Tours
New England and Europe
(800) 473-7040
www.bikeriderstours.com

Bike the Rockies
Canadian Rocky Mountain tours
(800) 938-7986
www.canusacycletours.com

Resources

Bike Vermont, Maine, Ireland, and Scotland
(800) 257-2226
www.bikevermont.com

Blackbeard Adventures
Variety of destinations in southern states
(888) 339-8687
www.blackbeardadventures.com

Carolina Tailwinds
Destinations in southeastern states
(888) 251-3206
www.carolinatailwinds.com

Ciclismo Classico
Specializes in Italian destinations; also has New England tours
(800) 866-7314
www.ciclismoclassico.com

Classic Adventures
Variety of domestic and international destinations
(800) 777-8090
www.classicadventures.com

Cog Wild Bicycle Tours
Pacific Northwest destinations
(800) 818-1902
www.cogwild.com

Crossroads Cycling Adventures
Long-distance fully supported tours
(800) 971-2453
www.crossroadscycling.com

Cycle America
Coast-to-coast rides along with national park tours

(800) 245-3263
www.cycleamerica.com

Dirt Camp
Mountain bike instruction and riding
(800) 711-3478
www.dirtcamp.com

Discover Vietnam
Destinations in Vietnam
(800) 613-0390
www.discovervietnam.com

Easy Rider Tours
Variety of European destinations
(800) 488-8332
www.easyridertours.com

Eden Excursions
Wisconsin's Kettle Moraine area
(414) 964-5822
www.edenexcursions.com

Escape Adventures
Variety of destinations specializing in the Pacific Northwest
(800) 596-2953
www.escapeadventures.com

Euro-Bike & Walking Tours
Variety of European destinations
(800) 321-6060
www.eurobike.com

Freewheeling Adventures
Variety of destinations in Canada and Europe
(800) 672-0775

Getaway Adventures
California wine country tours
(800) 499-2453
www.2getaway.com

Historic Adventure Travel
Archaeological and historical site tours by bike
www.historicadventuretravel.com

La Cima Tours
Variety of European destinations, specializing in Italy
(916) 641-2953
www.lacimatours.com

La Corsa Tours
Variety of European destinations for experienced riders only
(800) 522-6772

Lava Tours
Costa Rica bike and multisport tours
(888) 862-2424
www.lava-tours.com

Le Vieux Moulin Bicycle Touring
France destinations with private chef
(800) 368-4234
www.lvmoulin.com

Lunatours—For Women
Variety of international destinations for women only
(877) 404-6476
www.lunatours.com

Orchid Isle Bicycling
Hawaii rides
(800) 219-2324
www.orchidislebicycling.com

Peak Performance Camps & Tours
World-class coaching for riders of all abilities
(866) 806-6171
www.bikecamptour.com

Pedaltours New Zealand, Australia, and Vietnam
Variety of Southeast Asian destinations
(888) 222-9187
www.pedaltours.co.nz

Vermont Inn-to-Inn
Road and mountain tours
(800) 838-3301
www.inntoinn.com

Viva Travels
Variety of European destinations
(970) 926-8986
www.vivatravels.com

Wandering Wheels
Cross-country along southern route
(765) 998-7490
www.wanderingwheels.org

Western Spirit Cycling
Variety of domestic road and mountain biking destinations,
specializing in the Southwest
(800) 845-2453
www.westernspirit.com

Wild West Cycling Adventures
Destinations in southwestern states
(415) 456-8859
www.wildwestcycling.com

WomanTours
Variety of domestic and some international destinations for women only
(800) 247-1444
www.womantours.com

CROSS-STATE RIDES

Alabama

Bicycle Across Magnificent Alabama
www.bikebama.com

Georgia

Bicycle Ride Across Georgia
www.brag.org

Indiana

RAIN (Ride Across Indiana)
www.bloomington.in.us/~bbc/tours/rain/rain.html

Iowa

Register's Annual Great Bicycle Ride Across Iowa
www.ragbrai.org

Kansas

Biking Across Kansas
www.bak.org

Maryland

Cycle Across Maryland
www.cyclexmd.org

Michigan

Pedal Across Lower Michigan
www.lmb.org/palm

Minnesota

The Ride Across Minnesota
www.mstram.com

Missouri

Cycle Across Missouri Parks
www.mostateparks.com

Nebraska

Bicycle Ride Across Nebraska
www.bran-inc.org

Nevada

One Awesome Tour: Bike Ride Across Nevada
www.bikethewest.com

Oklahoma

Oklahoma FreeWheel
www.okfreewheel.com

Tennessee

Bicycle Ride Across Tennessee
www.state.tn.us/environment/parks

Wisconsin

Sprocket's Annual Great Bicycle Ride Across Wisconsin
www.bikewisconsin.org

OTHER GREAT RIDES

Great Divide Mountain Bike Route
www.greatdividecyclery.com/route.html

Hilly Hundred
www.hillyhundred.org

Hotter Than Hell Hundred
www.hh100.org

Race Across America (RAAM)
www.raceacrossamerica.org

Ride for the Roses
www.laf.org

Ride the Rockies
www.ridetherockies.com

Seagull Century
www.seagullcentury.org

Tour de l'Île de Montréal
www.velo.qc.ca/eng.htm

Packing Checklist

In addition to your usual helmet, gloves, shorts, jersey, and shoes, take the following on self-supported tours. Add more the farther you're traveling.

WEEKEND TOUR

Handlebar bag

Sunglasses

Sun/rain hat

Headlamp

Multiuse pocket knife

First-aid kit with antiseptic wipes, 12 sizes of adhesive bandages, gauze pads, antibiotic cream, medical tape (or duct tape), pain relievers, Bag Balm, Pepto-Bismol or comparable digestive soother, bee-sting kit (if you're allergic to bees), tweezers, needle and thread, first-aid literature

Camera

Journal and pen

Map

Compass or GPS

Pepper spray

Cell phone

On-the-bike snacks (see chapter 8 for the best types of munchies)

Rear Pannier

Rain jacket and pants

Extra shirt

Packing Checklist

Socks

Extra bike shorts

Hygiene kit with sunscreen, soap, razor, toothpaste, toothbrush, deodorant, and towel

Repair and tool kit with lube, duct tape, patch kits, a spare tube dusted with talcum powder, and a multitool with a chain breaker

On the Bike

Water bottle and cage

Pump (with at least two extra cartridges for a CO_2 pump)

Combination lock

Mirror

Camping Adds

Cookware and spoon

Camp stove

Food, including 8 to 16 ounces of rice, 8 ounces of pasta, four to six energy bars, packets of herbs and spices, four jerky packets (beef, turkey, salmon, and veggie), two hot chocolate packets, and one or two freeze-dried camp meals

Sleeping bag

Sleeping pad

Nylon tarp and rope

WEEKLONG TOUR

Second Rear Pannier

Extra jersey

Two more pairs of socks and underwear

Another pair of bike shorts

A good book

Five extra spokes

Spare brake/derailleur cable

Extra tube

Address book

Extra water bottles or a hydration system

Camping Adds

Campsite shorts

Double food

Sandals

Polypropylene top and bottom

Light tent

CROSS-COUNTRY TOUR

Seatbag

Waterproof oversocks

Insulated, waterproof gloves

Fleece pullover

Extra tire

More water

Bungee cords

Extra batteries for headlamp

Packing Checklist

Stamps

Swimsuit

Camping Adds

Water treatment tablets

Multiseason tent

Emergency blanket

INTERNATIONAL ADVENTURE

Two Front Panniers

Passport

Two more extra T-shirts

Insulated cold-weather tights

Hiking boots

Long pants

Dress shirt

Second extra tire

Spare brake

Up to 10 feet of brake/derailleur cable

Two more extra tubes

Water system (either a collapsible water container or a water filter)

More batteries

Additional maps and reading material

Photo ID

Toilet paper

Flat-Tire Cheat Sheet

Remove this page and stow it in your seatbag as a flat-repair Cliff's Notes.

1. If it's your rear wheel that flatted, click into the smallest cog. Shift into the hardest gear and turn the pedals so that the chain moves into the smallest cog. This makes it easier to remove and replace the wheel, because the chain is more out of the way.

2. Remove the wheel. Flip the quick-release (QR) and spin it five or six times to loosen it. Unhook the brake cable or flip the cable release to move the pads away from the rim. To remove the front tire, push it straight down. For the rear wheel, you'll need to push forward and down, angling the wheel to the left to allow the chain to come off the cogs.

3. Remove the tire and tube. With your thumb and forefinger, pinch the tire bead all the way around the wheel. Put the wheel on the ground between your feet. Grab the tire and press down, then pull it up, over to the side, and off the rim.

If your tire is harder to remove, the following three tips will help.

• Use tire levers. Slip the spooned tip of one tire lever between the tire and rim. Pry the second lever into the space between the first lever and the rim and tire. Lift the second lever to further pry the tire from the rim. Then push along the rim, moving the tire up and off. This technique works for most tires, but if a tire has a really tight bead, you may need to use three levers. Wedge the first between the tire and rim. Hook the other end into the spokes. Wiggle another tire lever into the space the first one made. Scoot it as far down the rim as you can, then hook the end of the second tire lever into the spokes. Use the third lever to pry the tire from there.

• Soap it down. If you have any soap handy or can slip into a bathroom and borrow a handful, coat the bead with the slippery stuff. This'll allow the bead to slip over the rim more easily and let the tire levers move into place. No soap? You can just use water from a bottle or hydration pack as a lube.

• Pinch and pull. Stretch the tire bead by pinching the sides together and pulling every section all around the rim. This move is similar to the one you use to take off a tire by hand, but you go all the way around the wheel pinching and pulling up the tire.

4. Find the damage. Run your hand around the inside of the tire to feel for glass or thorns, and visually examine the sidewalls of the tire and rim. Make sure the flat-causer isn't still lodged in the tire before you install a new tube. If there's nothing poking through the tire, find the hole in the tube by inflating it and listening for the air. If there are two pinch marks, you have a pinch flat that may have been caused by too-low pressure or from hitting an obstacle such as a pothole. Be sure to add more air next time.

While the tire and tube are off the rim, inspect the spokes to be sure none are poking through the rim tape, puncturing the tube. Usually you can tell by running your hand along the tape or looking for holes in the tape.

5. Put it back. Slip one sidewall of the tire back on the rim. For a tight tire, use the palms of your hands to push up and roll the tire into place. Put a tube in the tire, slide the other sidewall into place, and inflate the tire. When it's about halfway inflated, spin the wheel to ensure that the bead is seated. If the bead is not on the rim properly, there will be a bulge in the tire where it meets the rim. To fix, deflate, tuck in the bulge, and reinflate. Often, the bead doesn't seat properly because the tube gets snagged between the tire and rim. Deflate and pinch together the tire's sidewalls while wiggling.

Once it's inflated, slip the wheel into the dropouts and press the frame down on it to ensure it's in the frame correctly. Tighten the QR. Reattach the brakes. Before riding off, spin the wheel to be certain that it's still properly centered between the brakes and that the pads don't touch the tire.

Photo Credits

Pages 29, 92-93, 106, 107, 113, 114, 123, 124, 125, 126, 144, 155 (bottom), 157: © Mitch Mandel/Rodale Images

Pages 41, 153 (bottom), 160, 167, 173, 179, 180: © John Peters

Pages 48-49: Courtesy of Cannondale Bikes

Pages 108, 153 (top), 155 (top), 156, 158, 159, 164, 166, 168, 171 (top), 174, 175, 176, 178: © Rodale Images

Page 170 (top): Courtesy of Shimano

Page 170 (bottom): Courtesy of Campagnolo Corp.

Page 171 (bottom): Image provided by SRAM Corp.

Page 177: © Paul Schraub

Page 185: © Richard Price/Getty Images

Page 188: © Jerry Alexander/Getty Images

Page 191: © Skip Brown/National Geographic/Getty Images

Page 194: © Reuters/CORBIS

Page 196: © Dennis Marsico/CORBIS

Page 198: © Jan Butchofsky-Houser/CORBIS

Page 201: © Gregg Adams/Getty Images

Page 204: © Joseph Sohm, Visions of America/CORBIS

Page 206: © Pete Soloutos/CORBIS

Page 207: © Richard Hamilton Smith/CORBIS

Index

Boldface page references indicate photographs.
Underscored references indicate boxed text.

California wine country dream trip, 187–90, **188**
Camera, packing, 32
Camping
  clothing for, 37–38
  on cross-country tour, 39
  food for, 35, 38
  packing for
    campsite shorts, 37
    cookware, 35
    emergency blanket, 39
    food, 35, 38
    nylon tarp, 36
    polypropylene top and bottom, 38
    rope, 36
    sandals, 38
    sleeping bag, 35
    sleeping pad, 35
    spoon, 35
    stove, 35
    tent, 38–39
    water treatment tablets, 39
  pros of, 12
  on weekend tour, 35–36
  on weeklong tour, 37–38
Cancellations with tour company, 22
Carbohydrates, 118, 132–34
Carrying a load, training for, 104–5
Cell phone, 33
Century rides, training for, 109
Chainrings of touring bike, 51
Chains
  lubricating, 157–58, **157, 158**
  repairing broken, 174–76, **174, 175**
  wear of, 156–57, **156**
Chainstays of touring bike, 47
Changing lanes in traffic, 84
Charity tour, 14
Cleaning bike, 154, **155**
Cleats, replacing worn, 162
Climbing skills
  off-road, 96–97, 98
  touring, 70–71, 71

Clothing. *See also* Shirts
  campsite, 37–38
  for cold weather, 147–48
  everyday, 37–38
  gloves
    insulated/waterproof, 38
    mountain bike, 94
    touring bike, 52
  hat, sun/rain, 31
  hiking boots, 39
  mountain bike, 91, 94
  oversocks, 38
  pants, 39
  shoes, 53, 94
  shorts
    hygiene and, 112
    investing in padded, 45
    mountain bike, 91, 94
    packing extra, 33, 37
    touring bike, 53
  socks
    packing extra, 33, 37
    touring bike, 53
Cold weather
  clothing for, 147–48
  hypothermia and, 147
  preparing for ride in, 146–48, 147
  tour during, 16
Colorado Rockies dream trip, 200–203, **201**
Commuting to work on bike, 104
Compass, 29, 33
Cookware, packing, 35
Cooldown after training, 115
Cornering skills, 68–70, 69, 82–84
Countersteering, 75
Credit card, using on vacation, 13
Cross-country tour
  camping on, 39
  description of, 11
  dream trip, 205–7, **206**
  packing for, 38–39
    checklist, 219–20
  tour companies for, 206

M

Packing *(cont.)*
mirror, 34–35
oversocks, 38
pants, long, 39
pepper spray, 33
photo ID, 42
pocketknife, multiuse, 31
questions to ask about, <u>36</u>
rain gear, 33, 38
repair and tool kit, 34
shirts, extra, 33, 37, 39
shorts, extra, 33, 37
snacks, on-the-bike, 33
socks, extra, 33, 37
spokes, extra, 37
stamps, 38
storing items and, 42–43
strategies, 42–43
sunglasses, 31
swimsuit, 39
tire pump, 34
tires, extra, 38–39
toilet paper, 42
tour company and, 23–24
tubes, extra, 37, 39
water bottles, 34, 37–39
Pannier. *See* Rear pannier
Pants, packing long, 39
Partner
traffic riding and, 80
training with, 115, 117
Passing etiquette, 73
Pedals
clipless, 54
replacing, caution about, <u>161</u>
of touring bike, 54
Pepper spray, packing, 33
Photo ID, packing, 42
Physical problems and training,
avoiding, 112–14, **113**
Pocketknife, packing multiuse, 31
Preparing for the unexpected
bears, <u>143</u>
cold weather, 146–48, <u>147</u>
dogs, <u>142</u>
forest fire, <u>142–43</u>

high altitude, 148–49
hot weather, 141, 144–46
lightning, <u>142</u>
mountain lion, <u>143</u>
snakebites, <u>142</u>
tornado, <u>143</u>
wet weather, 139–41
Pretrip maintenance checklist
bolts, 152, **153**
brake pads, 158–59, **158**
cables, 154–56, **155**
caution about, <u>161</u>
chains, 156–57, **156**
cleaning bike, 154, **155**
cleats, 162
handlebar tape, 159–60, **159**
lubrication, 157–58, **157**, **158**
tires and tubes, 153–54, **153**
tools, 160, **160**, 162
Protein, 133
Pullover, packing fleece, 38
Pullup exercise, 107, **107**
Pumps, packing tire, 34
Purifying water, <u>136</u>, 137
Pushing bike, 97–98, <u>98</u>
Pushup exercise, 106, **106**

Q

Questions to ask
children on supported tour, <u>10</u>
do-it-yourself tour, <u>27</u>, <u>36</u>
packing, <u>36</u>
tandem tour, <u>9</u>
tour company, <u>19</u>
vacation choice, <u>6</u>, <u>7</u>

R

Race Across America (RAAM), 207
Rack eyelets, 54
Racks for mountain bike, 91
RAGBRAI (Register's Annual Great
Bicycle Race Across Iowa), 11
Rain gear, 31, 33, 38, <u>53</u>. *See also*
Wet weather

Touring bike *(cont.)*
  upright position and, 47, 50
  wheels of, 50
Tours. *See specific types*; Vacations
Traffic, riding in
  alongside moving cars, 81–82
  alongside parked cars, 84
  beginners and, 80
  changing lanes, 84
  crossing driveways or intersec-
    tions, 84
  giving warnings about, 73
  with group, 73
  looking ahead, 80–81
  with experienced partner, 80
  right of way, 81
  in rush hour, 84–85
  sidewalk riding and, 85
  turning, 82–84
Trail difficulty, knowing, 88–89
Trailer for mountain bike, 91
Training
  advanced program, 120–22, 121,
    123–26
  amount of, 109
  attitude toward riding conditions
    and, 127
  beginner program, 109–11, 111,
    115
    mistakes of, avoiding, 115
  benefits of, 103
  breathing technique and, 115
  for century rides, 109
  commuting to work on bike and,
    104
  cooldown after, 115
  for do-it-yourself tour, 109
  drafting and, 111, 115
  excessive, avoiding, 120–21
  exercises
    crunch, 108, **108**
    neck stretch, 114, 114
    pullup, 107, **107**
    pushup, 106, **106**
    reverse crunch, 123, 123
    reverse wrist curl, **113**, 113

Russian twist, 124, **124**
  superman, 126, **126**
  vacuum, 125, **125**
fitness test and, 109
food, 117, 121
formula for, 103
for hard-core touring, 103, 109
on hills, 120
hydration and, 110
intermediate program, 116–19, 116
interval, 120
log, weekly, 126–27, 128–29, 130
neck stretch, 114, 114
with partner, 115, 117
physical problems and, avoiding,
    112–14, **113**
skipping days and, 115
sleep and, 117
spinning cadence and, 117
strength training and, 121–22
stress-free, 110
stretching and, 110–11, 114
for supported group tour, 109
for terrain, 110
to carry loads, 104–5
two-thirds rule and, 110
warmup before, 115
Trips. *See* Vacations
T-shirts. *See* Shirts
Tubes
  packing extra, 37, 39
  patching, 165
  removing, 164–66, **164**
  riding without, 167
  tying leaking, **167**, 167
  wear of, 153–54, **153**
Turning skills, 68–70, 69, 82–84

U

U-lock, 30
Unweighting skills, 75
Uphill
  off-road riding skills for rocky,
    96–97, 98
  tour riding skills for, 70–71, 71